Finding Peace in a World of Worry

Bible solutions for stress and anxiety

by
DOUG BATCHELOR

Printed in the U.S.A.

This book is not intended to be or to replace professional medical advice. If you struggle with anxiety and depression, please seek professional counseling.

Cover by Haley Trimmer
Layout by Greg Solie • Altamont Graphics

ISBN: 9781580197236

Contents

Introduction

Have you ever felt utterly overwhelmed with worry?

Benjamin Franklin said, "Do not anticipate trouble or worry about what may never happen. Keep in the sunlight." That's easier said than done, isn't it? Worry can cast a profound shadow over our lives.

And there is certainly no limit to the number of things over which we can choose to fret, stew, and stress: our children, our health, our finances, our relationships, our material possessions, the unknown future—and, of course, our salvation.

Worry has become an epidemic in our culture and in our individual lives. The sad thing is that some people agonize so much about missing out or protecting what they have, they burn up considerable time and energy that they could be utilizing to create a fulfilling, joyful life for themselves and for others. All the good things the Lord has planned for them today slip right through their fingers as they fret about how things could be better and worry about the future.

In short: They're sinking while they're thinking.

Wouldn't it be nice if you could have someone do all your worrying for you? Well, in a very real sense, you can. The apostle Peter, a close disciple of Jesus, tells us to cast "all your care upon [Jesus], for He cares for you" (1 Peter 5:7).

Take heart! The Lord is intimately concerned with every aspect of your life, even the "small things." The Savior once stopped to explain that God's care for His creation is so broad and so deep, He is aware when a little sparrow falls to the ground. Jesus connected the dots for us: "Do not fear therefore; you are of more value than many sparrows" (Matthew 10:31).

It should come as no surprise to us, then, that the Bible often addresses the worries and anxieties that plague the human experience. And, thankfully, it offers solid, practical solutions not only for the worry itself, but also for the problems of life that trigger our worries in the first place. And that's what this book will explore.

But I should make one thing clear at the outset: This is principally written for someone who believes in God and has accepted Jesus as Lord and Savior. If a person is running from God, he has plenty to worry about—and I have no desire to offer that person an illusion of peace while he continues down the road to eternal loss. But, perhaps in reading these pages, even someone like this will be inspired to turn to the only One who offers a peace that passes understanding.

I pray that as you read this book, you will find more peace and less stress—that you will discover and experience how God's love can melt away every worry for the present and secure for you an eternal future.

—Doug Batchelor

Chapter 1

Are You Strangled by Worry?

The story is told of a man whose airline flight had been delayed due to a dangerous storm. He was already a nervous flier, but the threat of bad weather made his anxiety even worse. *What if lightning strikes the engine? What if the plane goes down?*

As he paced around the airport waiting for the storm to subside, his apprehension grew.

Eventually, he came across a vending machine offering $100,000 in life insurance. The travel policy would cover anything unfortunate that happened to him during his flight. The policy cost only a few dollars, and, worrying about his dear family having to live without him, he purchased one.

After obtaining his vending machine insurance policy, the man came across a Chinese restaurant in the airport and decided to grab a bite to eat. The food was especially tasty. Soon after, the storm outside began to dissipate. The man actually started to relax and even enjoy himself—that is, until he cracked open the fortune cookie.

The tiny strip of paper inside read:

Your recent investment will soon pay big dividends.

Well, that could make even the skeptics among us apprehensive —right?

It might be nothing more than a cute story, but it is true that worry seems to be a significant part of most people's daily mental processing. Indeed, did you know that the average person spends at least one-and-a-half years of his or her life steeped in focused worry? Yet we also know from studies that 80 to 90 percent of what people worry about never actually happens.

Mark Twain is credited with saying, "I am an old man and have known a great many troubles, but most of them have never happened." And Thomas Jefferson remarked, "How much pain they have cost us, the evils that have never happened." And it's true. Worry causes an incalculable amount of needless suffering.

But what exactly does it mean to worry? It means to agonize over disturbing thoughts or anxieties, resulting in fear, unease, or sleeplessness. It can involve feeling restless about something that has happened, but it also frequently involves feeling anxious about something that only *might* happen.

Imagination typically plays a starring role in worry. Sometimes we're tempted to fantasize potential catastrophes. Our minds sweep forward in time to build the most frightening possible scenarios and outcomes, inflating even minor things totally out of proportion. An old Swedish proverb says, "Worry often gives small things a big shadow."

However, worry is like a strenuous, exhausting exercise that builds no muscle. Jesus reinforced the uselessness of worry with a touch of humor by asking, Can worrying actually make you taller? (Matthew 6:27). The obvious answer is no.

Does that make you worry?

Choking on Worry

Perhaps we should look a little deeper at the word "worry." It appears to come from an old Anglo-Saxon word, *wyrgan,* which means "to choke or to strangle." Have you ever seen a person choked by their fears? Have you ever been choked by worry? I think we all have at one time or another.

Maybe you've seen a dog wearing a "choke" collar. It can be a handy device if you have a large, headstrong dog that you're trying to teach to bend to your will. The harder the dog pulls to get away from you, the tighter the chain gets around its neck.

There's also an apt expression about anxiety in the game of pool: "choking behind the eight-ball." The word "choke" is used in other games and sports as well. Basketball players are said to "choke" when they fail to make the easy free throw needed to tie the game; their anxiety that they could miss becomes compounded as all the fans and teammates depend on them to make the shot. Baseball players are said to "choke" because there's too much pressure to drive home the winning run.

Sadly, some people go through their lives constantly choking on worry. All their happiness, success, and joys are choked out of their lives by constant fretting, which leaves no room for anything else.

Jesus used a parable to illustrate the way in which worry can choke a person.

> A sower went out to sow his seed. ... And some fell among thorns, and the thorns sprang up with it and choked it (Luke 8:5, 7).

Some of the good seed fell among thorns, which choked out its life. This means that there are those who are still distracted by their worldly concerns even after they've heard the cleansing Word of God. The Bible is never able to be fruitful in their lives, and, as a result, they bear no fruit for God's kingdom. Why? Because they're so choked by worry concerning the cares, riches, and pleasures of the temporal life that they have no time to focus on what will change them spiritually and prepare them for the eternal kingdom.

How many Christians do you think experience this kind of choking worry? If we could just learn the lesson of simple childlike faith, we'd all have so much more peace in our lives. Not only would we be happier, we would also better reflect the love and character of God to others. In this book, I'm hoping to help build a bridge that will encourage you to do just that.

Of course, we all have a natural tendency to worry. In our fallen world, there are virtually millions of things a person can potentially choose to worry about. It's a very natural human habit to hyper-process our concerns, but that doesn't mean it's a good habit. Jesus told His followers, "No one can serve two masters; for either he will hate the one and love the other, or else he will be loyal to the one and despise the other. You cannot serve God and mammon" (Matthew 6:24).

The word "mammon" used in this passage is the word for riches and other wealth. Money and job security, which is the avenue of obtaining money, are typically listed among the top concerns that people worry about. But while "mammon" certainly may include money, it can also mean an abundance of "stuff." I like this translation: "You cannot serve God and an abundance of stuff."

The famed writer George Orwell once said, "Within certain limits, it is actually true that the less money you have, the less you worry." Well, the same can be said of "stuff." We tend to worry about our stuff—both the tangible and intangible things in our lives—which can easily distract us from the positive things of God.

Jesus goes on to say and, indeed, He commands us to *not* worry. But don't go start worrying about worrying too much! We'll take a closer look at these words later on.

Chapter 2

How an Ancient Riddle Offers Insight

About thirteen centuries ago in Ireland, three brothers stood together debating a philosophical puzzle. They posed a crucial question that many people are still asking today.

There are several versions of this story, but the one I first read told how a man named Caiman and his two brothers paused to talk one day on a place called Holy Island, which lies between the counties of Clare and Galway.

As they looked at a small stone church, they asked each other: "If you could fill this church with anything you wanted in order to be the most benefit to humanity, what would you choose?"

Each brother offered up a different solution.

The first brother said, "I would fill the church with all the gold in the world so that anyone who had a need could come at any time and receive help."

The second brother said, "I would fill this church with books so that scholars would come and learn all knowledge, and then go out and teach it to others. Anytime someone had a question, they could find the answer here."

But the third brother had a different perspective. He said, "I would fill the church with all the diseases in the world—everything that could cause harm. I would shut them tightly inside so that the people living outside these walls would be free of pain and illness, and they would be able to create a blessed life for themselves."

I share this story because it shows us a powerful and intriguing insight about how to limit worry in our lives. The solutions that each brother offered to this ancient puzzle actually reveal a model to help us design a new approach for peace of mind today.

First, let's look at what does *not* work. Even though this story is some 1,300 years old, most people today would give the same answers as those first two brothers. It's easy to think, "My life would be so much better if only I had more money." When we see headlines about lottery winners who end up discovering that their new life isn't as great as they first imagined it would be, many say, "Well, that wouldn't be *my* experience. If I had that much money, I know my problems would disappear."

Really? Solomon, one of the richest kings in history, said that with increased wealth comes much more stress and worry: "The abundance of the rich will not permit him to sleep" (Ecclesiastes 5:12).

Now think about how many people agree with the approach of the second brother. They think, "I'll be able to eliminate all of my problems if I just have enough knowledge. After all, look at how scientific advances have eliminated diseases that we once dreaded. Surely, with research, I will conquer my obstacles."

It's true that wisdom helps avoid and even resolve many problems, but it doesn't eliminate them. Knowledge alone will *never* be enough to remove worry. And any solutions we find will never bring lasting peace to our hearts. Someone even said "ignorance is bliss" because the more you know, the more aware you are of a multitude of other troubles in the world.

Every time we rely solely on money or knowledge to eliminate a problem, another problem pops up in its place. And that's what makes the solution of the third brother so intriguing to me. He went straight to the heart of the matter.

Digging Deeper

The third brother basically said, "Money and knowledge are great things in their proper spheres, but they don't go far enough in avoiding the things that really make us worry. We need to address the root cause. Instead of providing resources when trouble comes, I'm going to eliminate the things that cause worry in the first place by shutting them up inside the church. I'm going to give people a life free from these burdens."

Another way to look at the three solutions would be to update it to something we all dread: a vehicle that breaks down regularly. Would you rather …

1. Keep making enough money to pay for ongoing repairs?
2. Or maybe acquire the knowledge to perform the repairs yourself?
3. Or would you like to own a vehicle that never breaks down in the first place?

Obviously, the only thing that's going to keep you from worry is having a car that you know won't break down on you every time you try to start it up.

Now, let's look at this story in practical terms. How will it help make a difference in your life today? Well, you already know that it's impossible to eliminate all the problems that keep you up with worry at night. After all, Jesus told us that following Him doesn't guarantee an easy life: "In the world you *will* have tribulation; but be of good cheer, I have overcome the world" (John 16:33, my emphasis).

How do we do more than just read these words? How do we actually *replace* our worries with "good cheer"? And what about the words of the apostle Paul to the church members in Philippi: "Do not be anxious about anything"? (Philippians 4:16). Sometimes that seems impossible—even irresponsible.

When questions like these cross your mind, remembering the story of this ancient tale is a great place to start—especially as we begin practicing the solution offered by the third brother. You already know that you won't start living a better life just because you're making more money or earning multiple degrees.

But if you knew how to put away your worries so completely that they no longer had power to impact your life, think of the joy and freedom you would experience in your life.

The Bible reveals how to do this! By following the practical principles of God, you can build a toolbox of resources to address *anything* that you worry about. You can successfully cast away your worries and remove their power by storing them in the right place. You can live free from the constant sense of foreboding plaguing your life today.

In the chapters ahead, I'm going to share some fascinating insights and approaches that you may not have heard before. I'll give some scientific information about how to combat and neutralize worry and its worst effects on your mind and heart. And I'll share some fascinating stories from wise men and women who've learned the secrets of letting go of stress and taking hold of abundant joy and peace.

Most important, I'm going to show you how the Word of God gives you simple steps to deliverance—and unlimited resources of power, comfort, and hope. I'm going to share with you a wonderful collection of practical tools that God has shown me over the years—tools that will strengthen your faith and remove the choking power of worry.

So if you're ready to break that cycle once and for all, keep reading!

Chapter 3

You Are Designed for Freedom

On January 10, 1954, flight attendants welcomed passengers on board BOAC Flight 781, traveling from Rome to London, and the flight crew continued with their preflight checks.

This was the Golden Age of air travel, and Flight 781 offered a premium in-flight experience. The de Havilland aircraft harnessed its state-of-the-art design to fly higher and faster than any other passenger plane on the market.

When the aircraft door finally closed, twenty-nine passengers sat on board, including ten children who were returning to England for school after the Christmas holiday. The weather was perfect as the plane taxied into place for takeoff.

At 10:31 AM, the aircraft thundered down the runway and lifted into the brilliant blue sky above the Mediterranean Sea. While the plane climbed smoothly to 36,000 feet, passengers were offered tea and refreshments.

But exactly twenty minutes after takeoff, Flight 781 suddenly disintegrated in mid-air. Pieces of flaming wreckage plummeted into the ocean near the island of Elba.

There were no survivors.

Shock reverberated around the world. How did this modern aircraft fall out of the air on a beautiful sunny day? Was it sabotage? Prime Minister Winston Churchill decreed that no money or effort should be spared in solving the mystery.

After a complicated salvage operation and painstaking investigation, engineers finally discovered that the aircraft had a fatal design flaw: The windows of the airplane had square corners.

As the aircraft pressurized and depressurized during each flight, stress concentrated around the sharp corners of the square windows. Metal fatigue gradually resulted and, over time, the fuselage weakened. Eventually, under the concentrated pressure at altitude, it blew apart.

Because of this tragedy, all commercial airliners now have rounded corners on their windows. These corners evenly distribute the stress, and the aircraft structure remains strong. Maybe that's why God made eggs round; have you ever seen a square soda can?

Correct the Flaw

I sometimes think of this story when I hear someone say, "Christians should never be stressed!" It feels as though they're implying that experiencing stress is an improper response from a believer—or that all causes of stress will be cleared from the path of a faithful Christian.

They seem to overlook Bible verses that speak of believers facing trouble, fear, and even crushing discouragement:

"In the world you *will* have tribulation …" (John 16:33).

"Whenever I *am* afraid …" (Psalm 56:3).

"*When* my heart is overwhelmed …" (Psalm 61:2).

How do you resolve the tension between living by faith yet feeling fear—trusting God for perfect peace but experiencing stress in hard times?

Like everyone else, Christians face enormous trials—difficulties that bring uncertainty, pain, even bone-deep fear. They lose their jobs, go through debilitating illness, or experience wrenching family situations.

Are you supposed to pretend that these things don't bring anxiety to your heart? That doesn't seem honest; does it?

I believe there is a truthful *and* useful way to reconcile these questions. I would suggest that the Bible doesn't teach that Christians should never worry. Even Jesus felt anxiety in the garden of Gethsemane.

Rather, God's Word shows us that Christians need never *stay* stressed. In Psalm 23, David says, "Yea, though I walk through the valley of the shadow of death, I will fear no evil; For You are with me." Notice that David did not say there will be no dark valleys. The key is you do not camp in the valley; you go "through" the valley with God.

Good Stress vs. Bad Stress

Perhaps we should pause here to emphasize that not all stress is bad. Elizabeth Anne Scott, MS, in her acclaimed book *8 Keys to Stress Management,* writes,

> "Good stress," or what psychologists refer to as "eustress," is the type of stress we feel when we feel excited. Our pulse quickens and our hormones surge, but there is no threat or fear. We feel this type of stress when we ride a roller coaster, compete for a promotion, or go on a first date. There are many triggers for this good stress, and it keeps us feeling alive and excited about life.
>
> Another type of stress is acute stress. It comes from quick surprises that need a response. Acute stress triggers the body's stress response as well, but the triggers aren't always happy and exciting. This is what we normally think of as "stress" (or "bad stress"). Acute stress in itself doesn't take a heavy toll if we find ways to relax quickly. Once the stressor has been dealt with, we need to return our body to homeostasis, or its pre-stress state, to be healthy and happy.

> Chronic stress is another form of bad stress. It occurs when we repeatedly face stressors that take a heavy toll and feel inescapable. A stressful job or an unhappy home life can bring chronic stress. This is what we normally think of as *serious stress*. Because our bodies aren't designed for chronic stress, we can face negative health effects (both physical and emotional) if we deal with chronic stress for an extended period of time.

Stress itself is not a design flaw on God's part, especially in a world in which stressful situations exist. But a human flaw does appear when we park on the chronic worry and allow it to take root. Generally, you can walk over an anthill without getting bit; it's when you stand atop it for too long that you get eaten alive.

Worry concentrates stress exactly where it will do the most harm—just like the square windows on the de Havilland concentrated stress in the corners and caused metal fatigue. And just as the airline industry modified their design to rounded windows in order to safely redistribute the chronic stress, the Holy Spirit must reshape our thoughts to safely redistribute the stress we face in life.

We were never designed to live in a perpetual state of worry; in fact, we were designed for freedom. That's why you can be thankful that when stress enters your life, the Bible provides you practical ways to redistribute it safely.

Let's take a look …

Step 1—Act Immediately

The first step to proper distribution of stress is to recognize that we were never designed to carry it around in the first place. You were designed to *immediately* hand your stress to God.

> "[Cast] all your care upon Him, for He cares for you" (1 Peter 5:7).

"Cast your burden on the Lord, and He shall sustain you" (Psalm 55:22).

If we try to handle overwhelming worry in our own strength, we are operating with a design flaw. But we correct the flaw when we hand the burdens of our heart to God.

He is the only One with the power to carry them all victoriously. So keep in mind that we are not in charge of handling our hard times. God is!

God never worries. He does not nervously wring His hands and stress. He does not perspire with anxiety. He does not nervously pace the floor fretting over any outcome. He is the embodiment of peace. He is God. He sees the future with perfect clarity, and He's not worried. He has a thousand ways to resolve your problems when you can't see even one. He wants you to trust Him with your anxieties.

But mentally transferring our burdens into God's keeping may not always seem easy to do. I'm sure you have struggled with this at times. We might come to God in prayer, share the burdens of our heart, but then walk away still haunted by them when our prayer ends. We *want* to cast them upon the Lord and leave them in His hands, but what if we can't seem to stop thinking about them?

First, don't be discouraged! Just because we keep thinking about our situation isn't an indication that we've failed to hand the burden into His care. We may need to *repeatedly* bring urgent and desperate situations back to God.

A great way to do this is to simply present the situation to Him and ask for His help. Then repeat a Bible promise that affirms your faith. For example, you might pray, "Lord, I am so concerned for my daughter. She doesn't seem to acknowledge You in any way, and she's making choices that I fear will lead to pain and hard times down the road. Please be with her. Help me to trust her to Your love."

Then you could repeat 2 Timothy 1:12: "I know whom I have believed and am persuaded that He is able to keep what I have committed to Him until that Day."

Every time you find yourself worrying, repeat these steps. Bring the situation to God and repeat His promise, over and over. Do not allow stress to take root in your heart; instead, redistribute it by handing it to the God of all power.

Step 2—Words Matter

The second step that will help you to redistribute stress is to *change the words* you use when you talk about your challenges.

Too often, we use harmful, self-defeating phrases such as, "I can't handle much more of this," or "This is just hopeless," or "I'm such a failure." But you must abandon these negative statements immediately, because people are deeply and powerfully affected by our own words. We actually grow to become like what we think we are.

Someone who views themselves as a failure because of one unsuccessful situation can often superimpose that negative picture on everything else they attempt. And those who believe they are a failure in life tend to act in ways that affirm it, even if it isn't true. As a consequence, they usually don't turn out to be very successful.

Did you know that the Bible says that the words we use matter in every aspect of our lives? "As he thinks in his heart, so is he" (Proverbs 23:7). So you may be wondering how you can change the words you use yet still describe your situation honestly. After all, when a situation feels ominous, it seems foolish to try to pretend it's not a big deal.

I know what you mean because I feel that way too sometimes. But I also have a solution that works great for me. I stop using my own words to describe my situation, and instead I use the *words of Jesus*.

My words automatically fall short because my definitions are limiting. My perceptions are narrow. And I know that the devil will want me to define my problems in hopeless terms. So, I always want to view myself and my situation through God's eyes instead. No longer are we fearful casualties of disaster: "We are *more than conquerors through Him* who loved us" (Romans 8:37, my emphasis).

Only Jesus defines who we truly are. He pronounces that we are His children. "Beloved, now we are children of God" (1 John 3:2)—with full access to an inheritance of unlimited blessings. The Lord who created us and knows us better than we know ourselves pronounces us victorious sons and daughters of the Kingdom.

Words matter. When you think or talk about your difficult situations, you redistribute stress by using the words of God to define and view everything truthfully.

Step 3—The Psalm 42 Solution

When the enemy attacks you with concentrated worry, it can look as though there is no way out. We often feel despair even as we struggle to remember the promises of God. We might try desperately to pray but only get more discouraged.

So let me share the fastest, most powerful action I've found to properly distribute stress in such intense times. Psalm 42:5 offers a simple answer:

> Why are you cast down, O my soul? And why are you disquieted within me? Hope in God, for I shall yet praise Him for the help of His countenance.

The simplest way to triumph in your darkest moments is to praise God *before* you even see the answer. Power tends to flow when we praise the Lord *in advance.*

Remember the great story in Acts about Paul and Silas in prison? They'd been arrested and severely beaten because they were preaching the gospel. Then they were thrown into a dark cell and their feet were fastened in stocks.

Everything about their circumstances seemed hopeless. So what did they do?

> At midnight Paul and Silas were praying and singing hymns to God, and the prisoners were listening to them. Suddenly there was a great earthquake, so that the foundations of the prison were shaken; and immediately all the doors were opened and everyone's chains were loosed (Acts 16:25, 26).

Now, before we jump to the punchline of this story, let's take a moment to picture some of the other ways they could have responded to their scenario. Remember, their hands are chained to the stone cell, their feet immobilized in stocks, their backs stinging and burning from the stripes of the whip. Surely, it would have been easy for them to focus on their pain and cry out, "Lord, deliver us from our suffering!"

Or perhaps they could have pleaded for spiritual comfort. "Lord, don't abandon Your servants in this pit of despair. Comfort our hearts to know that You are with us. We have faithfully shared Your words, and now we need You to save us."

But that's not what they did first. They didn't pray for deliverance or strength or comfort. They didn't plead for God to step in with His mighty power and show His faithfulness. Instead, they put their faith into action immediately and began praising the Lord. They sang in the middle of their persecution.

Notice that the Bible doesn't tell us how they *felt;* it tells us what they *did*. They praised the Lord.

What happened? An angel came down after they praised God. I don't know about you, but it gives me amazing comfort to picture an angel, mobilized by my praise, hastening into my hardest situations with God's deliverance.

Praise doesn't wait for the answer, though. Of course, it's easy for most of us to praise God for victories *after* we win. It's difficult to praise God when we only see apparent defeat. But He is looking for people who will show faith by praising Him in advance. God looks for people who will take Him at His word.

When stress overwhelms you, when there seems to be no way out, remember that you were designed to praise God in every circumstance. Why? Because praise changes our focus. It clears away our *spiritual blindness* and opens our eyes to see the One who stands with us, ready to save. What King David wrote centuries ago still holds true today:

> I will bless the LORD *at all times*;
> His praise shall continually be in my mouth.
> My soul shall make its boast in the LORD;
> The humble shall hear of it and be glad.
> Oh, magnify the LORD with me,
> And let us exalt His name together.
> I sought the LORD, and He heard me,
> And *delivered me from all my fears*
> (Psalm 34:1–4).

Praise lifts your gaze from the insurmountable odds you face to the holy God seated on His heavenly throne in splendor and power. Paul and Silas were delivered when they praised. Praise will set you free even in the midst of bondage. So redistribute your stress with praise and thanksgiving to God.

Move the Needle

Albert Einstein famously defined intelligence in five ascending levels: Smart, intelligent, brilliant, genius, and simple. Now, as much as my wife, Karen, loves and supports me, I'm not sure where she'd put me on Einstein's scale. But if I were only sharing solutions for worry that I had engineered on my own, even if I were at the highest level of intelligence, this book wouldn't be worth much.

The value in these pages, and the results you *will* experience, come because these proven solutions are directly from the Word of God! When we face stress, only His design corrections truly set us free.

And yes: You weren't designed to live chained by stress in the prison of worry. You were designed for freedom. This is why Jesus said, "Fear not."

You may be living with a lifetime thought pattern of worry. You are in a "worry rut." You know that it is deeply entrenched. Anxiety may have become such an automatic response that you feel it's impossible to change.

So will you invest in a bold but simple strategy? When anxious thoughts come, choose to use these three steps and seek to worry five minutes less every day. That's all. Just five minutes less each day.

Now, you might be thinking that this hardly sounds like significant progress. How could worrying five minutes less every day really make an impact? Well, if you now currently spend one hour each day worrying, and you decide to follow this blueprint to worry just five minutes less every day, you would be worry-free in less than two weeks!

That seems like a pretty good deal for such a simple approach that anyone can do.

You don't need to lift the whole boulder to try to stop all your worrying immediately. Instead, just commit to worry a little less every day by using these three short steps. Want a shorter summary? Bookmark this page and come back every time you need to …

Step 1—Act Immediately

Whenever you feel anxious, remember that you're not designed to carry it—God is. He is the Lord of your life, *including* your stress. You weren't created to handle life's burdens in your own strength; you were designed to immediately cast your problems on the only One who can carry them victoriously. Read 1 Peter 5:7.

Step 2—Words Matter

You must change any self-defeating words you use when thinking about your situation. You want to use God's words because you will become what you think and articulate. In everything you face, God pronounces you a conqueror. Read Romans 8:37.

Step 3—The Psalm 42 Solution

Whenever you feel stressed, praise the Lord, even before you see answers. Ask the Holy Spirit to make praise your default response instead of worry. Praise shifts your focus to an almighty God. When you start actively looking for things to praise Him for, your eyes will be opened to see Him at your side more and more. Read Hebrews 13:15.

Chapter 4

Is Worrying a Sin?

Before going any further, we need to establish right now that not all worry is bad. Much of our worry is a perfectly normal emotion. In fact, a certain element of worry helps keep you alive, especially in a world full of sin and darkness. Of course, I'm not talking about choking anxiety and panic that paralyzes a person, but rather of that thoughtful apprehension of potentially negative consequences.

When my children were young, I wanted to impress upon them a healthy fear of playing near busy streets with speeding cars. I wanted them to look both ways twice before they crossed the road because there is an inherent danger involved. But the fear of traffic shouldn't have been keeping them up at night. I simply wanted them to have enough fear so as not to blindly chase a wayward ball bouncing onto a busy street.

I also remember worrying as a kid about getting my assignment done for class the next day. A little worrying in that department was probably a good thing; otherwise, I would've wasted time goofing off. I was guided into correct behavior by the fear of negative consequences of a failing grade. Of course, it wasn't my only motivation; I was equally eager for the praise of getting a high grade. Still, I worried a little about getting my homework done, and I survived.

So worrying isn't a sin in and of itself. (Stop worrying!) It is perfectly normal to encounter everyday problems and feel a little unease that motivates you to find solutions. You might visit worry, but don't camp on it. A little salt in the soup is good—but if you drink seawater, it will kill you.

Even the Spirit-filled heroes of the Bible worried about their problems.

You can be sure that Abraham was stressed when God asked him to sacrifice his beloved son Isaac. But he ultimately cast his burden on the Lord, and God strengthened his faith through this ultimate test.

Mordecai worried when the king issued a death decree for all the Jews in Persia. Wouldn't you worry about a genocide? So Mordecai fasted and prayed and then came up with a practical plan to deal with the problem at hand.

An Unfair Burden?

Now, you might ask: "Is it fair for God to ask me to not worry when I don't have His all-knowing foresight?" Indeed, while we can make educated guesses about the future, we don't know *for certain* what's going to happen in the future—even the next second. That uncertainty is what causes most of our anxiety. Yet as Christians, we need to learn to rest in the knowledge that God is in control of the universe and our lives.

Because God can see the end from the beginning—indeed, He *is* "the Beginning and the End" (Revelation 1:8)—He can effectively guide us onto the right path, so long as we're agreeable to trust His leading. He says, "I will instruct you and teach you in the way you should go; I will guide you with My eye" (Psalm 32:8).

What would happen to your worry if you embraced this promise with all of your heart? Yet the core question remains: Will you choose to trust your life to someone who knows your past, your present, and your future—and has your best interests in mind?

The Lord says, "Trust your worries with Me," because He knows that stressing, being anxious, fretting, wringing hands, and losing sleep aren't the ways to deal successfully with our problems. They actually make them worse, because we often throw reason out the window when bad things happen. We need to know how to commit our troubles to the Lord and allow Him to guide us to the right solutions.

But let's go back to our question, "Is worrying a sin?" Worrying is not in itself a sin, but left unchecked, it can become sinful worrying. Why is that?

Romans 14:23 says, "Whatever is not from faith is sin." In one sense, when we worry excessively, we are putting ourselves in the place of God—almost as if we believe we have all the power necessary to change our circumstances. That can be a form of idolatry. If we're spending so much time worrying about things so that we don't have time to consider God's guidance, it can mean that we're not trusting that His power is the only thing that can actually make the difference.

Notice that we need to have faith not only that God exists, but also that He will guide and support us as we make an effort to draw closer to Him:

> Without faith it is impossible to please Him, for he who comes to God must believe that He is, and that He is a rewarder of those who diligently seek Him (Hebrews 11:6).

Our heavenly Father is the source of every good and perfect gift (James 1:17), and He cares for His children. He longs to provide for you. He wants you to go to Him with your needs and then to actually rely on Him to supply those needs.

A Multitude of Worries

We've discussed it a little bit already, but what do people worry about? Well, just about *everything*. We worry about our food, clothes, relationships, and our children. We worry about money, gossip, and our reputations. We worry about our retirement. People who are single worry that they may never get married. People who are married often worry about staying married.

The list is almost endless.

In one poll, 36 percent of U.S. adults said that one of the biggest sources of worry is their job. Twenty-two percent said they worry about money. Ten percent said they worry about their children; five percent worry about their parents.

Five percent of people worry about their marriage. Actually, ten percent of women said they worry about their marriage compared to three percent of the men—averaging out to about five percent. It seems most men say, “If I don’t hear any complaints, our marriage must be fine.” It seems many women don’t feel that way.

Twelve percent worry about what others say about them, even though we can’t really do much when that happens. Ten percent worry about their health—of course, worrying about your health can make your health worse! More on that later.

Only five percent of people said they have no worries. Are you worried that you’re not one of them?

Whatever you worry about, it’s good for me to point out that only about eight percent of the things people worry about are actually worth worrying about. That means that of the things in which we invest our worry, more than nine out of ten are a big waste of time and emotional energy. It reminds me of a lady who once told me, “Don’t tell me worry doesn’t do any good. The things I worry about never happen.”

Sure—sometimes ignorance is bliss. Many people are anxious because of all the bad news they see on television or read online. It’s easy to become restless about government spending and bureaucratic waste or shocked by moral decline after yet another Hollywood scandal or when a sports icon tumbles from his or her pedestal. There’s never a shortage of political scheming to worry about either. Natural disasters—earthquakes in various places, tornados and unprecedented hurricanes—often seem to fill the headlines too.

That’s why limiting your consumption of negative news can help preserve peace of mind. The apostle Paul said that we should be proactive about keeping our thinking positive.

> Brethren, whatever things are true, whatever things are noble, whatever things are just, whatever things are pure, whatever things are lovely, whatever things are of good report, if there is any virtue and if there is anything praiseworthy—meditate on these things (Philippians 4:8).

However, even if you *do* watch the evening news a little too much, it doesn't mean you should be frightened. Jesus said, "You will hear of wars and rumors of wars." You would think wars and rumors of war would be reason to worry, wouldn't you? Yet Jesus, in the same verse, said, "See that you are not troubled" (Matthew 24:6). We regularly hear news about some dictator who keeps threatening to launch missiles at everybody, turning us all into glowing radioactive dust. Russian troops amass on the European border. Political problems and social unrest persist in the Middle East and Africa. So if we're not supposed to worry about a nuclear war, then what *are* we supposed to worry about?

Jesus was not worried.

Let's think about this. Some people worry all through their lives about staying alive, but then when their lives are nearly over, they have deep regrets. They worry about the things they didn't do. They spent all their time and energy worrying instead of enjoying the here and now of life. Corrie ten Boom, a woman who helped many Jews escape the Nazis, said, "Worry does not empty tomorrow of its sorrow; it empties today of its strength." How effective would she have been if she was consumed with worry about what might happen to her if she reached out to help the oppressed Jews in their time of need?

Worry can sap our vital forces, making it impossible for us to help others in need.

You have to make up your mind to trust God despite difficult circumstances. Ask yourself, "Do I trust God?" That's the core question only you can answer. But also ask, "Is God worried?" And, "Is God anxious about nuclear war?" No. He's not worried. Do you really picture God up in heaven with the veins bulging out of His forehead, dripping with perspiration and wringing His hands? Do you think He's saying, "What am I going to do now? Oh, no, I never saw that coming!" Is God worried about anything—or is He the epitome of peace? He may be sad, yes, but He's not worried at all in the sense that humans are worried.

He is omnipotent, all-powerful. With a God like that on your side, why worry?

Are You Worried About Death?

Most people are keenly aware that life is terminal. Knowing this, many of us fret about all the horrible ways that we could die. For instance, I made up my mind a long time ago that I would rather freeze to death than burn to death. (Of course, given the choice, I certainly prefer not to die at all. As comedian Woody Allen said, "I'm not afraid to die; I just don't want to be there when it happens.")

Worrying about all the possible ways you might die could give you an ulcer—and that could, theoretically, be the thing that kills you. Cancer, car wrecks, plane crashes, tornadoes, asteroid strikes—the gloomy options are limitless. It's a wonder that we can even sleep at night. Speaking of which, about ten percent of Americans die in their sleep. Then again, 25 percent die from heart disease. Ironically, worrying about a heart attack can contribute to a heart attack.

All this is why it is essential to have an abiding faith in God. Hebrews 2:14, 15, says that, through the death of Jesus,

> He might destroy him who had the power of death, that is, the devil, and release those who through fear of death were all their lifetime subject to bondage.

Amen! Perhaps that's why Leonardo da Vinci said, "As a day well spent brings happy sleep, so a life well lived brings happy death." Indeed, did you know that the Bible refers to death as a sleep from which you will awake? And for the Christian, it is a very happy resurrection! Assuming you are not afraid to go to sleep at night, that's a joyful promise that should end our fear of death—of that great void that comes when we die.

Tony Campolo, the famous Christian evangelical, once joked, "Why do we teach children to pray, 'If I die before I wake…'? We should be teaching them to pray, 'Lord, wake me up before I die!'" And I agree. If you're a Christian, your next conscious thought after death is waking up with a perfect, invigorated, glorified body with eternal bliss spread before you. Who would be afraid of that if they truly believed what the Bible said about life after death?

Here's what the apostle Paul said about it:

> For the trumpet will sound, and the dead will be raised imperishable, and we shall be changed. For this perishable body must put on the imperishable, and this mortal body must put on immortality (1 Corinthians 15:52, 53 ESV).

Thus, as da Vinci intoned, the most important thing for you is to live well. If your thinking is consumed with worry about dying, you're missing the point of living. How much better for the one who serves the Lord to recognize death as a God-designed "metamorphosis" to a new life? Let's see what Jesus said …

> Most assuredly, I say to you, unless a grain of wheat falls into the ground and dies, it remains alone; but if it dies, it produces much grain (John 12:24).

The book of Job echoes this thought: "You shall come to the grave at a full age, as a sheaf of grain ripens in its season" (5:26).

Don't Let Worry Make You Sick

There are serious drawbacks to excessive worrying. (But please, don't start worrying about them!)

First, worrying can damage your health. Proverbs 17:22 says, "A merry heart does good, like medicine, but a broken spirit dries the bones." It reminds me of this fanciful fiction:

> A man was walking to town and saw that Death was walking in the same direction. He got a little nervous, so he asked Death, "Where are you going?"
>
> Death replied, "I'm going to the town."
>
> The man asked, "What are you doing in town?"
>
> Death answered, "I've got an appointment to take a hundred people."
>
> The man ran ahead to the town and warned everyone, "Death is on the way, and he plans on taking a hundred people."
>
> Yet by the end of the day, a thousand people had died.
>
> When the man saw Death leaving the town, he said, "You lied to me. You said you were coming for only a hundred!"
>
> Death answered, "Sir, I kept my word. I took only one hundred. Worry took all the others."

Or it's like the man who goes to see a doctor for his yearly physical. The doctor starts with the basic health questions, asking, "How much do you weigh?"

"Oh, about 165 pounds," he says.

The doctor puts him on the scale, which reveals that his actual weight is 185 pounds. The doctor asks, "And how tall are you?"

"Oh, about six feet," the patient says.

The doctor checks and sees that he's only five foot, eight inches tall. Then the doctor takes his blood pressure and tells him it's incredibly high. "You could die," the doctor says.

"Well, of course it's high," the man responds. "What do you expect? I came in here tall and lean, and now you tell me I'm short and fat!"

Worry has a very real—and potentially deadly—impact on health. Nearly half of all adults, including Christians, suffer serious health effects due to worry. It has been estimated that as many as 90 percent of all doctor visits are due to stress-related complaints or disorders.

Anxiety can cause a vast range of physical symptoms, such as twitching, itching, trembling, muscle tension, headaches, sweating, dry mouth, difficulty swallowing, dental problems, abdominal pain, ulcers, dizziness, vision problems, rapid or irregular heart rate, rapid breathing, diarrhea, a frequent need to urinate, fatigue, irritability, sleeping difficulties, nightmares, decreased concentration, lower grades, hair loss, and other problems.

- Increased stress (anxiety) is a known factor that may lead to a heart attack, heart palpitations, and elevated homocysteine, another risk factor for heart disease.

- Stress has a detrimental effect on the parts of the brain responsible for planning, decision making, and reasoning. Less worry will keep you mentally sharp.

- Increased stress can elevate the levels of digestive acid, which can increase the risk of heartburn, ulcers, and irritable bowel syndrome.

- Additional worry can keep you awake. Having adequate rest is one of the most important factors in good health.

So be at peace … and live longer.

Mark Twain has been quoted as saying, "Drag your thoughts away from your troubles—by the ears, by the heels, or any other way, so you manage it; it's the healthiest thing a body can do; dwelling on troubles is deadly." Someone else said that for everyone who dies from a major misfortune, ten die from worrying about insignificant misfortunes.

Workaholics are often filled with remorse when they come to the end of their lives. If asked, "Do you have any regrets?" many will answer, "Yes! I spent my whole life worrying about working, worrying about providing. Now it's over, and I didn't really live. I didn't really enjoy my family. I didn't really see the places I wanted to see." Worrying can become such a habit, such an addiction, that it consumes your whole life. You become the walking dead, because you're never really living at all.

Helen Steiner Rice, the poet, wrote this insightful verse: "Worry. Why worry? What can worry do? It never keeps a trouble from overtaking you. It gives you indigestion and sleepless hours at night and fills with gloom the days however fair and bright."

We've already discussed a little bit about some things you can do to stop excessive worry—and therefore stop harming your body's health—but there's more to say about that in the next chapter.

Chapter 5

Beat Worry by Getting Off the Couch

One of the most practical ways we can combat the health risks of worry is through physical activity. Regular exercise can defuse tension and get more blood flowing to the brain, so we can think more clearly and rationally—often leaving us better capable of finding healthy solutions to the problems that are driving our worries.

Someone said, "A day of worrying is more exhausting than a day of work." If you've ever spent a day immersed in worry, you know how true that proverb can be. Worry drains away our store of physical and emotional energy.

This is why exercise is such a predictable way to beat stress, but it's only predictable because it's so effective. For instance, *The New York Times* reported that animal research reveals that exercise can affect serotonin—the "happy" brain chemical—as well as reduce the effects of oxidative stress. *Well and Good,* a health website, points out studies showing that those who participate in exercise interventions have lower anxiety levels than people who stay tied to the couch. "Several studies have found the effects of aerobic exercise to be initially similar to those of medication," Jeff Dolgan, an exercise physiologist at Canyon Ranch Hotel & Spa in Miami Beach told *Well and Good.* "However, in the long term, exercise seems to work better."

A simple walk in nature, surrounded by the peaceful evidence of its loving Creator, can be especially soothing. Many times, getting outside and breathing in the fresh air will bring you immediate relief and peace. So go out into nature and reflect on the things God has created for you to enjoy—all those beautiful reminders of His love for you.

Do You Want to Worry … or Witness?

Another tragic drawback to excessive worry is that it can damage a Christian's witness. Oswald Chambers, the great evangelist said, "Worry is an indication that we think God can't look after us." Jesus said,

> Do not seek what you should eat or what you should drink, nor have an anxious mind. For all these things the nations of the world seek after, and your Father knows that you need these things. But seek the kingdom of God, and all these things shall be added to you (Luke 12:29–31).

He's not saying that we should never think about our practical needs, but that we shouldn't be anxious about them. Jesus is saying we're no different than the unbelievers if we worry about these things all the time.

The famous Christian author Ellen White wrote,

> Do not fret, do not worry. By looking at appearances, and complaining when difficulties come, you show an enfeebled, sickly faith. Show your faith by earnest, cheerful work. The Lord is rich in resources. He made the world. He is never bound by circumstances. We need to look heavenward, in faith. Let us look to God, who has light, and power, and efficiency (*Review & Herald*, September 27, 1898).

God doesn't want you to be consumed with worry because it contradicts your faith. It contradicts your witness. Unbelievers are watching us all the time; they know we're Christians and that we believe in God, and if we're always fretting, why would they want our religion?

One of the things that brought about the conversion of John Wesley was his observation when traveling with Moravian Baptists, who possessed a remarkable peace during a raging storm at sea; they weren't afraid. And their immovable faith convinced him that something important was missing in his life.

Let's face it: Many people say they're Christians but don't live like they have faith. They live as if everything depends on them and nothing depends on God. But the Lord wants us to lean on Him, as Psalm 18:2 describes:

> The Lord is my rock and my fortress and my deliverer; my God, my strength, in whom I will trust; my shield and the horn of my salvation, my stronghold.

What would happen to our witness if we traded our worries for that kind of Rock-solid faith? How many more people would be attracted to the God we serve?

But our worrying doesn't just affect the people outside our home. Worrying can affect our families, including our children.

After church one day, a family invited visitors home for dinner. As they were finally gathered around the table, ready for lunch, the mother of the family asked the daughter, who was five years old, if she'd like to have prayer. The little girl seemed to be quite nervous. She hadn't been asked to do that before. She said, "I'm not sure what to say."

The mother said, "Well, just pray like Mommy prays."

So the little girl folded her hands, closed her eyes, solemnly bowed her head, and said, "Dear Lord, why did I ever invite all these people over?"

Funny, yes, but serious too because impressionable kids really do closely watch and listen to adults. If they see that you are constantly stressed and worrying, they will reproduce your worrying in their own lives.

A dear friend of mine once shared an amazing story with me. As a contractor, he took his family up to Alaska during a construction boom and did very well for himself. They lived the good life for a good while, but then the bottom fell out of the market. It hit his family hard. Here he was with a wife and three children—and financially overextended. Almost overnight, they had no money for house payments and utilities. They had nowhere to go, and they even started running out of food.

Of course, you usually don't run out of food overnight. It starts out with you eating macaroni and cheese. But pretty soon, it's just macaroni and butter, and then it's macaroni and salt—and then you're out of macaroni.

My friend and his wife are Christians, and they said, "Look, the Lord knows that we need food. He's promised He will not let us go hungry. We read it right here in the Word that, 'If you then, being evil, know how to give good gifts to your children, how much more will your Father who is in heaven give good things to those who ask Him!'" (Matthew 7:11).

They made the firm decision to teach the kids faith, to be a witness to them. They had no idea from where God was going to get them some food, but they decided to ask the Lord. They knelt down as a family and prayed for His help.

What happened next? While they were still on their knees praying for food, the doorbell rang. At the door was a neighbor who worked for an airline. She said that because of bad weather, her flight had been canceled. "We've got all these extra meals for the flight that will go bad if we don't eat them; could you guys use any?" She offered them stacks of prepared in-flight meals, which they gratefully accepted, sticking several in the empty refrigerator. My friend said, "We ate all that airline food over the next few days."

What do you think that experience did for the kids' faith when they saw their parents praying for food—and then the doorbell rings and there's food? Their trust in God surely skyrocketed! The Lord has done those kind of things for me as well—absolute miracles. So you can rely on Him to provide the basics, such that you worry a little less.

Christians are supposed to be people of faith, but if we spend our lives worrying, how will that draw others to the Lord?

Folks don't want to know how to worry; everyone does that well. We're all experts in that department. But if we meet someone who knows how to put their faith in God and genuinely rely on Him, that can be inspiring.

It can even be life-changing.

Do You Want to Worry ... or Worship?

Two old friends met together for lunch to catch up. "How are things going in your life these days?"

The other replied, "Well, my house is in foreclosure, I lost my job, my medical insurance has been cancelled, and my credit cards are maxed out."

"Wow!" the first man exclaimed. "How are you coping?"

"I'm not worried," the friend said. "I've hired a professional worrier to worry for me."

"A professional worrier? What's that costing you?"

"He charges $50,000 a year."

The first gasped. "Where in the world are you going to come up with the money?"

"I don't worry about it," the friend explained with a wink. "That's *his* job!"

Wouldn't it be nice if we had someone to take care of all our worrying for us? In a sense, we do, and the even better news is that it's totally free.

Now, I'm not suggesting that Christians can live irresponsible lives and then demand that God gives them peaceful attitudes. Rather, that chronic worry is not part of God's plan for faithful believers. He wants to handle all of our worries and to permanently set us free from them. You might try writing down some of the things you're worried about and give them to God. Say, "Lord, You're my professional worrier. I'm giving my worries to You." Beyond that, He's given us a tremendous resource for learning not to worry: His Word!

And with that in mind, let's see how the Living Word tackled worry.

Chapter 6

Lessons from the Savior

Jesus teaches us how to not worry by providing some keen and inspiring lessons from nature. Let's consider how listening to Him will help us better manage our anxiety about, well, all kinds of stuff.

For instance, He says in Matthew 6:26, "Look at the birds of the air."

Now, I remember when I first read this passage, I thought, *I've got all these problems—big problems—and You're telling me, Lord, to look at the birds? I don't want to look at the birds. Birds don't worry like me because they don't have the same problems I've got.*

But Jesus knew what He was saying. He said, "Look at the birds of the air, for they neither sow nor reap nor gather into barns." You see, humans often get through the bad seasons by thinking ahead. We worry about the future and plan for it. Of course, there's nothing wrong with planning. Take a farmer, for example. He sows and weeds and puts the produce into storage to better prepare for the next growing season.

Still, Jesus pointed out that birds don't worry about things like we do. Have you ever seen a bird with a suitcase? When a bird decides to fly south, she just does it—without worrying about what to pack, where to go, or where to find food and shelter. Yet her needs are provided to her by the Creator. Birds seem to be largely carefree creatures. They wake up and fly and sing. And if it's raining, they find a dry spot under a branch. Birds enjoy life and simply take it as it comes.

Jesus is saying, basically, "Look, I see the sparrow when it's hungry. And I feed it. A sparrow does not fall to the ground without the notice of your heavenly Father." (See Matthew 10:29.) And then He reassures us in Matthew 10:31, "Do not fear therefore; you are of more value than many sparrows."

When Jesus sent out the apostles to preach, He pretty much told them to go as they were without taking any provisions. He wanted to especially impress upon them that God would supply their needs. "He commanded them to take nothing for the journey except a staff—no bag, no bread, no copper in their money belts—but to wear sandals, and not to put on two tunics" (Mark 6:8, 9).

Jesus wanted His disciples to learn a specific lesson about putting all their faith in the Father. And did He take care of them? Absolutely! Jesus has promised His disciples—then *and* now—that He "will never leave you nor forsake you" (Hebrews 13:5). Yet we often remain committed to being experts at worrying about stuff rather than relying on Him.

Many years back, I got on a passenger flight to St. Louis for a weekend speaking engagement. After boarding the plane, I realized that I had forgotten my phone charger, and my phone battery was down to 20 percent. I found myself fretting about this several times during the flight. My work often requires me to keep in frequent contact with the office. Besides, others were already expecting my call. I also wondered, "How would I call my wife through the weekend?" After I checked into the hotel and got to my room, I knelt down and prayed to thank God for a safe trip—and to help me figure out a solution to my phone charger problem.

When I opened my eyes, I was looking straight ahead at the electric outlet on the hotel wall, and I noticed that there was something plugged in it. *Could it be?* Yep! It was a charger someone evidently left behind. But would it fit my phone? Back then, there were dozens of adapter sizes for mobile phones. I thought, "What are the chances?" Well, it turned out it was the same Motorola brand as my phone and the charger fit perfectly!

I used it that night to charge my phone and the next day I turned it in to the front desk.

I did all of that worrying on the plane for nothing.

Jesus Shows You How to Trust

Christ also drew the attention of His followers to the flowers. He said, "Why do you worry about clothing? Consider the lilies of the field, how they grow: they neither toil nor spin" (Matthew 6:28). Jesus pointed our eyes to the bright and cheerful. Beautiful lilies don't have fretful looks while laboring over what they will wear.

Today, we can get clothes pretty cheap. But in those days, people spun their yarn and wove their clothing by hand, which required many hours of work. As a result, their clothing was comparatively expensive. As a matter of fact, people would sometimes use their cloak as a down payment on a debt. Samson, for instance, paid off a bet with clothing (Judges 14:19).

Clothing is, of course, a necessity for protection against the elements, but especially so in Bible times. People, including Jesus, wore an outer garment. At the cross, the Roman soldiers gambled for this robe. It was something of value. Yet Jesus told His disciples,

> Why do you worry about clothing? Consider the lilies of the field, how they grow: they neither toil nor spin; and yet I say to you that even Solomon in all his glory was not arrayed like one of these (Matthew 6:28, 29).

Let's face it: There are some incredibly beautiful flowers out there; no human can duplicate with their looms the delicate beauty of flowers.

I was in Hawaii once and had the opportunity to see an incredibly rare flower after climbing to the top of the volcano Haleakala; the flower is called silversword, which lives at altitudes of over 6,900 feet; it flowers just once in its lifetime. This round, succulent plant with sword-like silvery leaves stands less than two feet high. On top of the volcano, the plant frequently faces freezing weather and powerful windstorms, yet it's a survivor, often living fifty years or more. When it is mature, the silversword has a great burst of energy and sends up a tall spike covered with beautiful, brilliant, maroon-colored flowers, lasting for just a few weeks. It goes out with a bang. It lives half a century, flowers, and then dies. It seems to bloom just for the glory of God and the pleasure of a few volcano climbers.

Jesus makes my point:

> If God so clothes the grass of the field, which today is, and tomorrow is thrown into the oven, will He not much more clothe you, O you of little faith? (Matthew 6:30).

He says, "If God cares enough to feed the sparrows, if He cares enough to clothe the flowers, and you are made in His image, why are you worried? I'll take care of you too." Just as He cares for the flowers and the birds, just as He cared for the disciples that He sent on mission trips, Jesus cares for you today.

You have two choices. Will you worry, or will you worship?

Worry Less, Yes—But Plan Responsibly

Let me take a moment to clarify something important that I mentioned briefly. Although we should avoid worrying, it doesn't mean we shouldn't plan.

When God asks us to not worry, He doesn't ask us to never think ahead. He's not asking us to just go skipping recklessly through life without a care in the world—to have no objective and to be unconcerned about anything at all. That would be irresponsible! God does want us to use our heads to think, and there are places in the Scriptures that speak to us about planning.

Here are some examples:

"The plans of the diligent lead surely to plenty, but those of everyone who is hasty, surely to poverty" (Proverbs 21:5). We should plan carefully, while always seeking wisdom from above.

Proverbs 13:16 tells us, "Every prudent man acts with knowledge." Consider also Proverbs 14:8: "The wisdom of the prudent is to understand his way," to look ahead, "but the folly of fools is deceit." And in Proverbs 11:14, we find, "Where there is no counsel, the people fall; but in the multitude of counselors there is safety."

Jesus, too, referred to planning when He said, "Which of you, intending to build a tower, does not sit down first and count the cost, whether he has enough to finish it—lest, after he has laid the foundation, and is not able to finish, all who see it begin to mock him, saying, 'This man began to build and was not able to finish'?" (Luke 14:28–30).

Planning is an important strategy of life. God is practical in that way. But note that there is a difference between being aware there is a problem and thinking about a resolution—and worrying incessantly about the problem. Winston Churchill astutely said, "Let our advance worrying become advance thinking and planning."

While worrying can drain our energy, the right kind of planning can build energy and momentum. It's a much better use of our brain power.

Notice, however, that there is a right way to plan. The apostle James writes,

> Come now, you who say, "Today or tomorrow we will go to such and such a city, spend a year there, buy and sell, and make a profit"; whereas you do not know what will happen tomorrow. … Instead, you ought to say, "If the Lord wills, we shall live and do this or that" (James 4:13–15).

God expects us to make plans, but we ultimately need to submit all those plans for Him to direct because He sees the bigger picture.

Chapter 7

Don't Let Worry Drown Your Dreams

An Arab chief once told a story of a spy who was captured and then sentenced to death by a Persian general. This army general had the strange custom of giving condemned criminals a choice between the firing squad or "the big, black door." As the moment for execution drew near, the offender was brought to the general, who asked him the question, "What will it be: the firing squad or the big, black door?"

The spy hesitated for a long time. It was a difficult decision. He chose the firing squad. Moments later, shots rang out confirming his execution. But the general turned to his aide and said, "They always prefer the known way to the unknown. It is a characteristic of people to worry about the unknown. Yet we gave him a choice."

The aide asked, "What lies beyond the big, black door?"

"Freedom," replied the general, who confessed, "I've known only a few brave enough to take it throughout the years."

In nearly every way, worry is the diametric opposite of faith. A believer is to live by faith and walk by faith—to believe, to dream, and to pray for big things. But this often will require trusting God with the unknown.

The most successful people in life are those who aren't afraid of some risk—responsible risk, sure, but risk nonetheless. People who are always worried about stepping out of their comfort zone to take a new job, move to a new town, or invest in a new venture often go through their lives living in the mundane. Dreams are often drowned in the ocean of fear.

God frequently wants to give you the desires of your heart—see Psalm 37:4, for instance—but many are too paralyzed by fear of the unknown to make a change. Don't let worry keep you from experiencing the life God wants to give you:

> I know the thoughts that I think toward you, says the LORD, thoughts of peace and not of evil, to give you a future and a hope (Jeremiah 29:11).

Too Little or Too Much?

Jesus said, "One's life does not consist in the abundance of the things he possesses" (Luke 12:15). But you wouldn't know it by the average neighborhood in America.

Have you ever driven down a street in your community and saw homes with two-car garages, but both cars are parked outside? They were likely parked that way because their garages are filled to the brim with stuff.

I think it was Ben Franklin who said, "Abundance destroys more people than want." It's interesting to consider that although there are many people who worry about what they don't have, there are millions who worry about what they *do* have.

You have probably noticed the fad called "tiny living." Some people say that because of all our consumption, we produce too much carbon, which is detrimental to our environment. (I'm not making a case here for climate change one way or the other; this is a spiritual lesson.) They say we need to reduce our carbon footprint, so we need to start living smaller.

Part of their reasoning lies in a statistic that says that over the past 50 years, the average American home has increased in size by 1,000 square feet. Yet during that same time, the number of people in the house has gone down from 3.1 people to 2.5 people. So we've got fewer people living in bigger houses—and those houses are brimming with stuff!

A report in *Forbes* magazine about the "tiny house" phenomenon says that buying these tiny houses is a bad investment. It's a fad that ultimately doesn't make sense. Statistics demonstrate that the people who buy them are selling them for bigger homes within a few years. Sometimes they don't even make it a year because a law of life says you will fill whatever space you have. Move into a bigger house, wait a few years, and watch what happens. You will likely fill whatever space is available to you, and if you live in America, you may even rent extra space to store the overflow.

Yet for most people, possessions they thought would make them happy actually eat away at their happiness. This is especially true for Christians, who should know better. They determine that they can't go on a mission trip because who's going to take care of their stuff? You can actually become a prisoner to your things, spending your weekends oiling and maintaining and guarding your stuff when you could be visiting with your neighbors and giving Bible studies.

The Bible says that contentment is a great gain (1 Timothy 6:6). If we can be content and satisfied with a little bit, everything else is a plus. Worry becomes a thing of the past. The apostle Paul reminds us,

> We brought nothing into this world, and it is certain we can carry nothing out. And having food and clothing, with these we shall be content. But those who desire to be rich fall into temptation and a snare, and into many foolish and harmful lusts which drown men in destruction and perdition (1 Timothy 6:7–9).

Notice that word: "drown." How many Americans today are drowning in possessions and all the debt that comes with obtaining and maintaining their trove of junk?

In the same passage we find, "For the love of money is a root of all kinds of evil." Money is not evil, but the love of it leads to evil. We worry the most about the things we love the most. "Some have strayed from the faith in their greediness and pierced themselves through with many sorrows" (v. 10). My dad typically drank himself to sleep every night, but he was a wealthy man. Why? Because he had so many worries. Solomon said, "The abundance of the rich will not permit him to sleep" (Ecclesiastes 5:12). They are literally worried about stuff!

I remember reading a true story about two men in a fishing boat floating in very cold water off the coast of Vancouver. Their boat rammed into something and began to take on water, and soon it started to sink. The men threw their life raft out into the freezing sea and climbed into it—*and* that's when they noticed there was still a thick nylon rope securely connecting the life raft to the sinking boat. They scurried around to see if they could find a knife in their raft, but there wasn't. They knew they didn't have long.

Talk about being anxious! Out of desperation, they started *chewing* on the rope. They had to gnaw through the bulky nylon before their main boat sank, or it was going to pull them down and they would drown in the ice-cold water. They had to take turns chewing, because their jaws got sore fast as they gnawed at the rope. About an hour later, sure enough, they broke through the rope just as the boat slipped beneath the surface.

Like those desperate men, some people are so tethered to a mountain of stuff and are being drowned by all they have, they can't live the life God wants them to have—a truly abundant life.

Please forgive me for quoting Kris Kristofferson and his song "Me and Bobby McGee." One line in that popular folk tune goes, "Freedom's just another word for nothin' left to lose." In some ways, that's true. When I was a hippie wandering the country, I remember picking up my backpack and saying, "I wonder what state I'll visit today." I wasn't worried about what I was leaving behind. Fewer possessions meant greater opportunities.

My wife, Karen, and I met a fellow when we were diving in Hawaii. He was a scuba photographer who traveled the globe. He said, "When I travel, I don't take much with me." Sure enough, all he had brought on this trip was a little carry-on bag and a pass from an airline that allowed him to go anywhere in the world. He'd leave from one country, taking along his camera, toothbrush, and a few other things, and he'd go wherever he wanted.

I confess that I envied the freedom with which he could travel the world. He told us about all the exotic places he visited, and he said, "When I get there, I can buy the food and clothes that I need. I don't have to worry about anything lost in baggage." Traveling light through life can have similar great benefits.

People often think happiness is going to come from having more, but it's not true. It's a myth. I am not advocating for minimalism; I own way too much stuff to do that. But I've learned an increase of stuff generally does not increase your joy or your peace. Frequently, the opposite is true.

Furthermore, having more doesn't make you more valuable. That's another myth. Our value never changes in the eyes of God. The Bible says that those with great abundance often have a more difficult time entering the kingdom of heaven.

> It is easier for a camel to go through the eye of a needle than for a rich man to enter the kingdom of God (Mark 10:25).

Why? It can be a challenge for those who are comfortably wealthy to perceive their need of God.

Another myth is that more things will make you more popular. Actually, having wealth can make others resent and envy you. You become a target, and you don't even know who among your friends are really friends.

Some believe that more things will make them more secure or that more things will bring them greater contentment. Usually, if you're not content with what you have, more will not bring you contentment; you'll soon discover there's something else that you don't have and you'll be discontent again. Or your neighbor will have something that you don't have, and you'll feel compelled to compete.

Someone once asked the multimillionaire Nelson A. Rockefeller how much money it takes to make someone happy. His answer was telling for a rich man: "Just a little bit more."

Isn't it better to have the contentment we read about in 1 Timothy 6:8: "Having food and clothing, with these we shall be content"? God promises that He "is able to make *all* grace abound toward you, that you, always having *all* sufficiency in *all* things, may have an abundance for every good work" (2 Corinthians 9:8, my emphasis).

Have you noticed how many "alls" there are in that verse?

God provides *all* this that you "may have an abundance for *every* good work." God is willing and able to give you everything you need to do His work. He is not going to send you out into the world to do His work and then refuse to supply you with what you need to do it.

Chapter 8

Don't Let Worry Distract You

Another problem with worrying is that it can be a distraction from the things that are most important. This is illustrated in an experience that Jesus had while visiting some friends in the town of Bethany.

> [Jesus] entered a certain village; and a certain woman named Martha welcomed Him into her house. And she had a sister called Mary, who also sat at Jesus' feet and heard His word. But Martha was distracted with much serving (Luke 10:38–40).

Notice that word: "distracted."

Have you ever been worried to distraction while entertaining several guests? You're going from room to room, always thinking of something you forgot to do in the last room. You say, "I have to put more chairs in the living room," and then, "Oh, I need to watch what's on the stove so that it doesn't boil over!" You've also got to set places at the dinner table for all the people, but then the doorbell rings and you have to greet the next guest. Martha was in this kind of situation as she coordinated a large dinner for Jesus and His disciples.

As I was writing this section, my wife said to be careful; we should acknowledge our need for all the Marthas in the world—especially when there's a potluck. So, yes! I love the Marthas out there; if you want to get something done, give it to them to do and it will get done.

But that gift to serve can also become a problem if it gets out of control. When people are perfectionists and things get hectic, they worry. If they've got everything mapped out and put in its place, they feel great. "I've got it all covered now," they think. But if things start to move in the wrong direction—if the unexpected or unplanned suddenly happens—they find themselves on the verge of a meltdown. And they want others to worry with them.

That's what we see happening when Martha went to Jesus to protest.

In the meantime, Mary sat at Jesus' feet and eagerly listened while He taught. She was drinking in the Word with a warm heart. But Martha had a houseful to feed, and she wanted her sister to help. Martha was glaring at her sister—giving her "the eye"—snorting every time she walked through the room to get another casserole for the table.

She even thought, *"Now, Jesus is becoming an accessory to her irresponsible behavior. Look at all I've got to do!"* So she stopped and tapped her foot, folded her arms, and said, "Lord, can't you help me? Don't you care that my sister has left me to serve alone? Look, she's just sitting there. Tell her to get up and help me!" (See Luke 10:40.)

Look closely at how Jesus responded, however, for He is speaking to you and me here as well. He said, "Martha, Martha," as though saying her name once was not enough. Can you picture Jesus shaking his head with a smile and saying, "Martha, Martha"? He was speaking to the hostess politely and with a concerned, selfless heart. "You are worried and troubled about many things," He acknowledged (v. 41).

Do you know a Martha? Are *you* a Martha? Do you ever worry as Martha did? The only difference is the *what* you worry about.

I try to take a brief nap almost every day because I find I accomplish a lot more writing (and other things) than sitting at my desk for ten hours straight. But while I was lying down one day, I started thinking about everything I could be doing, and my heart started racing, and it was almost like a mini-panic attack. I thought, *"Oh, I've got so many messages to prepare and articles and letters to write. How am I ever going to get it all done?"*

But then I remembered: *"After twenty-five years as a president of a global ministry and thirty-five years of pastoring, remarkably, I'm still alive. And it seems like all those other responsibilities that have come up over the last few decades somehow got done—and the ones that didn't get done didn't kill me. I will probably survive."* Then I fell asleep.

Every problem in life falls into one of two main categories: the ones you have some control over, and the ones you have no control over. If you have no control over some predicament, it does not make sense to worry about it. If you do have some control, there's no sense worrying about it—just focus on the solutions to get the problem under control.

People like Martha, people who like to have everything under control all the time, need to pray that famous serenity prayer:

> God, grant me the serenity to accept the things
> I cannot change
>
> Courage to change the things I can
>
> And wisdom to know the difference.

The things that we worry about today, sometimes we look back and think: *"You know, God has brought me so far and worked out so many things in the past. And I wasted all the joy and peace and good witness that I could have had during that time worrying about the things that I didn't need to worry about. God always took care of it."*

King David put it this way, "I have been young, and now am old; yet I have not seen the righteous forsaken, nor his descendants begging bread" (Psalm 37:25). As an old man looking back across his incredible life, David recognized that God had always provided.

Let's go back to Jesus at the home of His friends. He said, "Martha, Martha, you are worried and troubled about many things. But one thing is needed, and Mary has chosen that good part" (Luke 10:41, 42). What did Mary choose? She chose to sit and hear the Word, and she worshiped Jesus. Do you want to worry—or do you want to worship?

We all need to sit at the feet of Jesus. By choosing "that good part," we find a Burden-bearer who will carry all our troubles for us. Cast your troubles on Him, because true worship will evaporate our worries.

Stop Worrying About the Past

The famous author Fulton Oursler once wrote, "Many of us crucify ourselves between two thieves: fear of the future and regret for the past."

Millions of people worry about what has already happened, even though they can't do anything about it. Bad decisions, failed investments, disastrous relationships—there's no end to the list of sad things you can conjure up and pine over. But since we haven't figured out a way to go back in time, there's no real point in stressing. Worry will never change history.

While regret over the past can help us avoid repeating a mistake, left uncontrolled, it can wreak havoc on our future happiness. Hours, days, or weeks spent feeling regret for a past mistake is almost always counterproductive. It can impede us from moving on with our lives. Letting go of the past keeps us from wallowing in regrets that drown out our dreams. The inventor Alexander Graham Bell said, "When one door closes, another opens, but we often look so long and regretfully upon the closed door that we do not see the one that has opened for us."

What about you? Have you ever spent endless hours worrying about past mistakes? Or perhaps you've come away from a difficult conversation and can't stop thinking about what you should have said or shouldn't have said. Perhaps you made a bad decision last year and can't stop rehashing it.

How can you learn to cope with regret? Simply acknowledge that it was a mistake and that it is a valuable learning experience. Then make the best of the here and now.

I like Thomas Edison's attitude; he saw every failed experiment as a kind of discovery. "I have not failed. I've just found 10,000 ways that won't work."

The pain of failure can be one of the most valuable learning experiences in life. Write it off as a valuable lesson for the future, and then move on. It's in the past; you can't change it—so you have to move forward.

Humans make mistakes; "we all stumble in many things" (James 3:2). When you become a Christian, you are born again, becoming a new creature. We must embrace that old things are passed away and all things become new in our hearts and lives. Stop worrying about mistakes the old you made. God has forgiven you; now forgive yourself—unless you think your judgment is more important than God's!

Continuing to worry about the past is futile, and it often ends in discouragement for the future. The Bible advises us to forget "those things which are behind" (Philippians 3:13). Stop wasting your time and energy wallowing in regret. "Remember not the former things, nor consider the things of old. Behold, I am doing a new thing" (Isaiah 43:18, 19 ESV).

Stop Worrying About What Others Think

I mentioned earlier the power of words. A lot of folks spend their lives preoccupied with what others think about them. Some are even worried about what other people think of their religious piety. That's why many people pray to be seen, give to be seen, and fast to be seen. (See Matthew 6.) But it's all empty show.

Or maybe you know people who worry too much about what other people are saying about them on Facebook, Twitter, or some other social media platform. They are worried about gossip, about their reputations. Here's a little tip from Ecclesiastes 7:21, 22:

> Do not take to heart everything people say, lest you hear your servant cursing you. For many times, also, your own heart has known that even you have cursed others.

Now allow me to give you a more modern translation:

> Don't worry about what everyone says. You're going to hear negative things said about you, even from those close to you, and you've probably done the same thing.

People tend to talk a lot, but the more we talk, the better the chance we will say something irresponsible. King Solomon said, "In the multitude of words sin is not lacking" (Proverbs 10:19).

I've even heard about a website that will do a search to find out who is talking about you online. That could drive you crazy! If you could hear what people are thinking about you, that would probably be even worse for your self-esteem. But in the big picture, this should not matter. It's what God thinks about you that is important!

Don't draw your value from people. Jesus tells us the same thing. In Matthew 5:11, He says, "Blessed are you when they revile and persecute you, and say all kinds of evil against you falsely for My sake." (Just make sure you live in such a way that it's indeed said falsely!) When people are saying false things about you, when they're ridiculing you and gossiping about you, Jesus not only says that you're blessed, He says you should rejoice!

> Rejoice and be exceedingly glad, for great is your reward in heaven, for so they persecuted the prophets who were before you (v. 12).

Now, do you rejoice when you hear people say false things about you? I have done that very thing a few times when I saw that I was being ridiculed because I took what I believed to be a biblical position. I even received a magazine that had my picture on the cover; the headline called me a false prophet. But I didn't worry about what it said. Why? Because I knew I was being ridiculed for preaching the Bible truth. After all, Jesus said, "Woe to you when all men speak well of you, for so did their fathers to the false prophets" (Luke 6:26).

Doesn't Jesus also say that if you're living for God, people are going to say negative things about you? "Blessed are you when men hate you, and when they exclude you, and revile you, and cast out your name as evil, for the Son of Man's sake" (Luke 6:22). He adds,

> If the world hates you, you know that it hated Me before it hated you. If you were of the world, the world would love its own. Yet because you are not of the world, but I chose you out of the world, therefore the world hates you (John 15:18, 19).

And not only do some people obsess about what others say, some are deeply worried about what they themselves are going to say. One of the greatest anxieties folks struggle with is when they are faced with public speaking.

But the promise for this is actually included in three of the Gospel books—Matthew, Mark, and Luke. Here is Luke's version:

> When they bring you to the synagogues and magistrates and authorities, do not worry about how or what you should answer, or what you should say. For the Holy Spirit will teach you in that very hour what you ought to say (12:11, 12).

After preparing a sermon, I try to not worry about it. I do my best to prepare well, of course, but then I have peace. I do pray that God will help me communicate His message, and that His Holy Spirit will speak through me so that it's not just some preacher talking.

Not long ago, I was speaking with a friend who is not a believer. I was praying all along, *Lord, help me know what to say.*

And God suddenly took the conversation in a new direction. I wasn't prepared for the response I got from this guy. He opened up about spiritual things, and we started talking religion. Don't worry about what you should say; instead, be genuine and let the Holy Spirit guide you in what you're supposed to say.

I was preaching one Sabbath and, after the sermon, a lady came up to me looking very distraught. She said, "Pastor Doug, I'm so glad that you did the closing prayer. I was supposed to do that prayer."

I hadn't looked in the bulletin, but sure enough, it said that someone else was supposed to do it. So I said, "I'm so sorry! I didn't see it in the bulletin."

But the lady had been so nervous and fretting all night about praying in public that it ruined her time at church! She said to me, "You know, I didn't hear anything you said during the sermon because I was so afraid about what I was going to pray." She was worried—and all for nothing, because I ended up saying the prayer anyway. She spent the whole sermon in turmoil; the devil got her so distracted with worrying that she wasn't able to sit at Jesus' feet.

You might have heard the funny story about the Christian in the coliseum. Every time the emperor threw him to the lions, the lions would refuse to eat him. At first, a lion would run over to eat him, but the Christian would whisper in the lion's ear and the lion would run off. This happened two or three times, and, finally, Caesar called the believer over and asked, "You have to tell me what you are doing. Every time that hungry lion comes near you, you say something that seems to make it lose its appetite."

The Christian said, "I just tell the lion that it'll be expected to say a few words to the crowd after it eats me."

Have you ever panicked about prayer? When I was a new Christian in a Bible study group, the pastor would sometimes say, "Let's all take turns praying." So we'd kneel in a circle and go around in turn. I was always so afraid about what I was going to say that I couldn't hear anyone else's prayer. Or the pastor would say, "We're going to read a Bible passage. Let's go around the circle and all take turns reading a verse." I never heard what anybody else read because I was so afraid that when my turn came to read my one little verse—at a time when many words in the Bible still intimidated me—that I was going to sound ignorant. I was so scared that it hijacked my blessing.

Some people are petrified about what to say, but it doesn't help to be worried. It only makes things worse. Put your trust in the Lord.

One Good Reason to Worry

Returning to something I mentioned at the beginning of the book: Is there a time a person *should* worry? Yes. Everything that God said about the promises and not having to worry, He's saying to those who have accepted Him. If you haven't accepted Him, perhaps you should worry.

Hebrews 10:26, 27 explains: "If we sin willfully after we have received the knowledge of the truth, there no longer remains a sacrifice for sins, but a certain fearful expectation"—isn't that worry?—"of judgment, and fiery indignation which will devour the adversaries." If you are turning your back on God and refusing to follow Him, then I hope you don't have peace. Why would you want someone to be comfortable on their way to destruction? So, I do think that there is a proper time to worry.

The Bible says that there is no peace for the wicked (Isaiah 48:22); Isaiah actually says this twice in his prophecy. And Revelation 16, speaking of the lost, says, "They blasphemed the God of heaven because of their pains and their sores, and did not repent of their deeds" (v. 11). These people in rebellion against God really have something to worry about. But as believers, we live by faith. If we have faith in the Lord, we have an entirely different worldview.

CHAPTER 9

Let His Blessings Bury Your Burdens

Marcus Tullius Cicero, the Roman philosopher, said, "A person who is to be happy must actively enjoy his blessings." And indeed, one of the best ways to avoid the pitfalls of worry is to count your blessings.

You might even start a gratitude journal. Take a minute every day to write down those things for which you're thankful. Almost all of us, whatever our situation, have something for which we can be grateful. It might be food in our pantry, the love of family, or an answered prayer. Try to think of two or three blessings each day and put them down on paper.

Then when things are going downhill and you're worried, read through the list and see how much God has given you—how much He has already blessed you. I'd like to share another interesting quote from the classic book *Steps to Christ* by Ellen White:

> Some are always fearing, and borrowing trouble. Every day they are surrounded with the tokens of God's love; every day they are enjoying the bounties of His providence; but they overlook these present blessings. Their minds are continually dwelling upon something disagreeable which they fear may come; or some difficulty may really exist which, though small, blinds their eyes to the many things that demand gratitude.

The devil works to inflate your problems to make them appear bigger than reality. The passage above concludes with:

> The difficulties they encounter, instead of driving them to God, the only source of their help, separate them from Him because they awaken unrest and repining.

People in this situation are overwhelmed with worry, and it's a waste of energy. God already knows about the things that you need and is waiting for you to come to Him and ask for help and guidance. That's why the apostle Paul said,

> Be anxious for nothing, but in everything by prayer and supplication, with thanksgiving, let your requests be made known to God; and the peace of God, which surpasses all understanding, will guard your hearts and minds through Christ Jesus (Philippians 4:6, 7).

E. M. Bounds writes: "Paul's direction is very specific, 'Be careful for nothing.' Be careful for not one thing. … for any condition, chance or happening. Be troubled about not anything which creates one disturbing anxiety. Have a mind freed from all anxieties, all cares, all fretting, and all worries. Cares divide, distract, bewilder, and destroy unity, forces and quietness of mind. Cares are fatal to weak piety and are enfeebling to strong piety. What great need to guard against them and learn the one secret of their cure, even prayer!

> "'Day by day,' the promise reads,
> Daily strength for daily needs
> Cast foreboding fears away;
> Take the manna of to-day."
>
> —*The Possibilities of Prayer*

Early in the eighteenth century, the city of Leningrad was laid out in a beautiful location. The problem was that a number of large rocks deposited by an ancient glacier had to be removed. A particularly massive piece of granite was lying directly in the way of the principal avenue, and bids were advertised for its removal. All of the proposals submitted by contractors were extremely expensive because there were no modern mechanical means for removal, no hard steel for drilling or cracking the stone, and no dynamite yet invented—only inferior black powder.

Before the contract was awarded to the lowest bidder, an insignificant-looking peasant appeared and offered to remove the boulder for a fraction of the sum and half the time quoted by the other bidders. Since the government ran no risks, the peasant was authorized to try his luck.

He assembled a small army of other poor farmers with spades and hefty logs. First, they used the large timbers to prop up against the side of the enormous bolder to prevent it from rolling, and then they began digging an immense hole next to the rock. After two weeks, when the crater was deep enough, the props were knocked away and the boulder slowly rolled out of sight into its deep grave—where it rests to this day below street level. The hole was then covered with dirt, and the rest of the earth was carted away. And the peasants? They were able to live comfortably for years on what they earned.

Have you made a monument of your burdens and regrets—like a constant "stone of stumbling and a rock of offense"? (Isaiah 8:14). They loom large as a constant reminder and as an obstacle to a peaceful and productive life. Perhaps you should dig a hole in God's abundant mercy and bury them. This is what the Lord does with our sins.

> You will cast all our sins into the depths of the sea (Micah 7:19).

> I will be merciful to their unrighteousness, and their sins and their lawless deeds I will remember no more (Hebrews 8:12).

When you confess and repent of your sins, God buries them in the depths of the sea and sets up a no-fishing sign. Why would you want to focus on your past failures when God has promised that He will remember them no more?

Bury your burdens in the blessings of His love!

He Will Provide

Jesus said to His disciples,

> Do not worry about your life [that's a command] what you will eat or what you will drink; nor about your body, what you will put on. Is not life more than food and the body more than clothing? (Matthew 6:25).

Again, He doesn't mean that we shouldn't give a thought to the basics of life; rather, we shouldn't *be anxious* about those things.

Isaiah 33:16 tells how God cares for the needs of the righteous:

> He will dwell on high; his place of defense will be the fortress of rocks; bread will be given him, his water will be sure.

When the children of Israel were led by the Lord out into the wilderness, did He give them food? Did He give them water? Did He preserve their clothes? After their forty years of going through the wilderness, God pointed out that He wanted them to look back and remember that their shoes and their garments did not wear out (Deuteronomy 8:4).

God took care of them. He provided for all their needs, and He will do the same for you. Jesus feeds the birds; He clothes the flowers—so don't worry about what you're going to eat or drink or what you're going to wear. He really does take care of us.

Of course, this is with the understanding that we diligently do what we can humanly do to acquire the basics. Work, plan, and live responsibly, but then trust your heavenly Father for what you cannot do for yourself.

When you are tempted to worry, remember this wonderful passage from the book *The Desire of Ages*:

> The continual worry is wearing out the life forces. Our Lord desires them to lay aside this yoke of bondage. He invites them to accept His yoke; He says, "My yoke is easy, and My burden is light." He bids them seek first the kingdom of God and His righteousness, and His promise is that all things needful to them for this life shall be added. Worry is blind and cannot discern the future; but Jesus sees the end from the beginning. In every difficulty He has His way prepared to bring relief. Our heavenly Father has a thousand ways to provide for us, of which we know nothing. Those who accept the one principle of making the service and honor of God supreme will find perplexities vanish, and a plain path before their feet.

Do you believe His promises? When you're praying, "Oh, Lord, I don't know how anyone, even You, could solve this problem," God says, "What do you mean? I've got a thousand options at hand!" We might not see any of those options, but He's got a thousand ways to provide for His children. Trust in that truth.

Chapter 10

Jacob's Challenge

I once heard a humorous sermon illustration about a man who came out of an office building in Chicago to find a policeman writing him a ticket for double-parking. The officer asked, "What in the world possessed you to do this?"

The man answered, "Well, whenever I go to the dentist, I always double-park because it gives me something to think about. If I worry about getting a ticket, it keeps me from worrying about the drill."

Perhaps, in a similar way, some people purposefully create additional problems to distract themselves from some of the more frightening worries in their lives, but the Bible has a much more effective solution.

Scripture tells about a time when Jacob encountered a big problem. You read about it in Genesis chapter 32. He was making his way back to the Promised Land; he had left it empty-handed, but God had blessed and prospered him since. He now had two wives, two surrogate wives, and eleven kids. He was going home, but his brother Esau, from whom Jacob stole the birthright, also heard that he was coming back. Esau was likely afraid that Jacob was coming home to actually claim the inheritance he had sold to his younger brother.

A messenger came to Jacob and said, "We came to your brother Esau, and he also is coming to meet you, and four hundred men are with him" (Genesis 32:6). Now, a large group of mounted men usually meant an army coming to fight. Jacob had women and children and flocks to tend, so he was not prepared to fight a battle.

Jacob was greatly afraid and distressed (v. 7).

Can you blame him? Wouldn't you worry about your family if you thought an army was coming to wipe them out? So what did Jacob do?

Well, if you've got a problem, how do you deal with it?

Make a plan.

God gave you a brain, so use your brain. Of course, you should always ask Him for wisdom when formulating any plan. "If any of you lacks wisdom, let him ask of God, who gives to all liberally and without reproach, and it will be given to him" (James 1:5).

Then, of course, use the wisdom He has given you. Try to have a plan moving forward and say, "Lord, this is what I've come up with. If You've got a better plan, please show me. In the meantime, I'm doing this." God will often show you a different option if you're sincere.

As for Jacob, he divided his family into two companies, reasoning, *If Esau comes to one company and he attacks, the other company may escape. Perhaps some will survive. Let me split them up.* Then he prayed, "O God of my father Abraham and God of my father Isaac, the Lord who said to me, 'Return to your country'" (Genesis 32:9). He was essentially saying, "God, didn't You promise that You'd take care of me? Didn't You tell me that through my descendants the Messiah would come? You told me it was time to come back to Your land, and I'm following Your instruction."

He claimed the promises of God!

But the Bible says that Jacob then wrestled with God. Sometimes you've got to wrestle with the Lord to take care of your anxiety until you can trust fully in Him. Jacob said, "I will not let You go unless You bless me!"

When you have problems, be honest with yourself and with God. Tell the Lord that you are worried. Tell Him that you don't want to worry because He doesn't want you to worry. Remind Him of the promises in His Word—not because He needs to be reminded, but because you do. You need to be specific and claim particular promises in God's Word. Take hold of them, grasp them, and don't let go. Tell the Lord, "I'm casting my cares upon You."

I imagine that you have your own particular worries and that you're plugging those into this equation right now. Well, let's consider the outcome of Jacob's situation. Did God take care of Jacob? By the time the two met, brother Esau had a heart change and actually hugged Jacob!

Choose to Walk on Water

You don't know how God is going to take care of your problems. You may not be able to think of even a single viable solution, yet the Lord has an infinite assortment of ways to solve all your problems. So worrying about them actually gets you nowhere. Doesn't it make sense to trust in God, the one who can provide the solution you need?

You have heard the story of Peter walking on water. The disciple was surrounded by a storm that would make even a fisherman nervous, but as long as he had his eyes on Jesus, he was able to do the impossible—he walked on water. You can also have peace in the midst of a storm as long as you keep focusing on the Lord.

When Christ was sleeping in the boat and His terrified disciples woke Him up, He asked, "Why are you afraid? Where's your faith?" He was saying that even a storm on the open water shouldn't rattle our faith. Storms may test our faith, but they should never destroy it.

At first, Peter was looking at Jesus when he was walking on the water. But the instant he took his eyes off Jesus, he started sinking. When he stopped looking at Jesus and started focusing on the waves and the wind, afraid for his own life, he started to worry. He lost faith.

If you focus only on the problem and you don't look at the Lord, you will lose faith. The reason David was able to conquer the giant Goliath is that he did not look at how tall Goliath was. He looked at how big God is.

One time, John Wesley was walking with a friend who was fretting about everything under the sun. And as they were walking along, Wesley looked over into the field next to the road and saw that there was a cow looking over the stone wall. And he asked his friend, "Do you know why that cow is looking over the wall?"

His friend shook his head.

Wesley said, "Because he can't see through the wall. You're trying to look through your problems. Instead, you need to look over your problems."

Someone once said that you should start every day by opening the window of heaven and say, "Lord, I'm Yours today, and my problems are Your problems because I'm your child." Will He take care of you? You can count on it!

When Peter began to focus on the storm, taking his eyes off Jesus, he began to sink. In desperation, he turned back to Jesus and called out in desperation, "Lord, save me!" Jesus took him by the hand and pulled him from a watery grave.

Jesus then guided Peter back to the boat and asked, "Why did you doubt?" Often, the reason we fret is because we take our eyes off Jesus—we lose sight of Him because of the wind and the waves of our lives. They consume our physical senses, and then we let them consume us spiritually. We focus too much on the problem. Again, this doesn't mean you should go through life oblivious, but you need to make sure that your faith is hanging on Christ. Superglue your focus on the Savior.

This Scripture passage urges us to fix our eyes upon Jesus:

> Since we are surrounded by so great a cloud of witnesses, let us lay aside every weight, and the sin which so easily ensnares us, and let us run with endurance the race that is set before us, looking unto Jesus the author and finisher of our faith (Hebrews 12:1, 2).

The King James renders it this way: "fixing our eyes on Jesus." When we fix our eyes on the Lord, He will not only keep us from worrying, He will save us.

Laugh a Little

The Bible says there is indeed a "time to weep," but there is also "a time to laugh" (Ecclesiastes 3:4). Yes, laughter is a great form of stress relief, and that's no joke. I can't tell you how many times in my life I have been able to better manage stressful situations because I saw something humorous in everyday life—such as the church sign that read: "Don't let worry kill you off. Let the church help!" Oops!

A report from the Mayo Clinic says that while a good sense of humor can't cure every ailment, data shows many positive things laughter can do for our bodies and minds. For instance, when you start to laugh, it doesn't just lighten your load mentally, it actually induces positive short-term chemical changes in your body. Laughter can:

- Stimulate organs (heart, lungs, brain) by enhancing your intake of oxygen-rich air; in doing so, it increases endorphin release in your body.

- Activate and relieve your stress response; a good laugh cools down your stress response. The result? A good, relaxed feeling.

- Soothe tension by stimulating circulation and muscle relaxation, both of which can reduce some of the physical symptoms of stress.

Laughter isn't just a quick pick-me-up, though. It's also good for you over the long term. Laughter may:

- Improve your immune system. Negative thoughts manifest into chemical reactions that can affect your body, bringing more stress into your system and decreasing your immunity. In contrast, positive thoughts can actually release chemicals that help fight stress and potentially serious illnesses.

- Relieve pain. Laughter may ease pain by causing the body to produce its own natural painkillers.
- Increase personal satisfaction. Laughter can also make it easier to cope with difficult situations and can also help you connect with other people.
- Improve your mood. Many people experience depression, sometimes due to chronic illnesses. Laughter can help lessen your anxiety and may make you feel happier.[1]

The Power of a Song

One of the most powerful things you can do to cope with anxiety is to sing. Many of the Psalms of David were written while he was enduring tremendous stress and difficulties.

The Bible tells about a time when Israel, ruled by King Jehoshaphat, was being invaded by three enemy armies. Greatly outnumbered by adversaries, Jehoshaphat was naturally worried, but after being counseled by a prophet, his confidence returned. He boldly instructed the priests to lead the army in songs of praise as they marched into battle:

> Do not be afraid nor dismayed because of this great multitude, for the battle is not yours, but God's. … You will not need to fight in this battle. Position yourselves, stand still and see the salvation of the Lord, who is with you (2 Chronicles 20:15, 17).

Jehoshaphat then appointed those who would sing, and he sent them into the battle in front of the soldiers. When they

1 Adapted from *Mayo Clinic Guide to Stress-free Living* by Amit Sood, 2013.

lifted up their voices and sang praises to God, their enemies turned on each other and wiped themselves out so that there wasn't a man left standing.

> When they began to sing and to praise, the Lord set ambushes against the people of Ammon, Moab, and Mount Seir, who had come against Judah; and they were defeated (2 Chronicles 20:22).

The enemy was defeated by songs of praise! Who would have predicted that? When His people followed His direction, God won the battle for them. They never needed to worry about what the outcome would be.

And what about the way that the walls of Jericho were brought down? It was through "special music." The army of Israel shouted and played their trumpets, and the walls collapsed.

Remember, when Paul and Silas sang hymns in prison, an angel rocked the jailhouse with an earthquake that set everyone free. So praise God in song *even* when you can't see a way out of your predicament. It will lift your spirit when you sing songs that honor Him, and He loves nothing more than to act on your behalf when you step out in faith!

You might be thinking, "Singing is the last thing I want to do when I am worried." Have you ever tried to sing a happy song when you're feeling troubled? Either you're going to get mad at the song—or you'll start changing your attitude. One time I was worried about yet another travel problem. I was returning from a mission trip overseas. My group's flight was canceled, and I was very depressed about it. One bubbly member of our group, however, was very optimistic. He said, "Let's sing 'He's Able.'"

I thought to myself, *"Oh, not now. I don't want to sing. I want to worry."* Like when Solomon said, "Like one who takes away a garment in cold weather, and like vinegar on soda, is one who sings songs to a heavy heart" (Proverbs 25:20). It might seem like an annoyance, but if you start singing and praising God anyway, you may find your worry taking a backseat. Music has enormous power, and that power can be used for our benefit. It can be a game changer in your battle with worry.

Delegate and Distribute

I once read about a terrible warehouse fire in Oakland, California, that killed nearly forty people. The authorities later determined that it was due to an overloaded circuit. Too many appliances were plugged into a single outlet, which was designed to handle only a few electric amps. And because the occupants did this, some wires heated up and shorted out, causing a spark that ignited the deadly fire. The blaze spread rapidly, and tragically, there was only one exit downstairs. Most people were trapped upstairs and died from smoke inhalation.

A terrible and tragic throng of death and destruction was all caused by a single overloaded circuit.

Likewise, when you try to carry by yourself everyone's problems and all of the problems of tomorrow, and the week after, and the month after that, and you multiply one on top of the other, you will eventually overload your circuits till they begin to smoke and burn out. God didn't design us this way. That's why Jesus said in His discourse about worry, "Sufficient for the day is its own trouble" (Matthew 6:34). That's an old way of saying that God gives you enough grace to deal with the problems of today.

What about those in positions of leadership? Maybe you are a manager in an office, a pastor of a church, or a mother of a large family. You carry the concentrated worry of many problems. The story above has a special message for you. Electricity is a safe and wonderful power that can make our lives much easier, but the distribution of appliances must be evenly spread among many circuits so that they don't overheat. That means you have to learn to delegate. Invite people and family members around you to take on some of your tasks. Don't try to do it all yourself.

You might be one of those people who says, "If you want something done right, do it yourself." Yet with that mentality, you will never teach your children to do the dishes. You have to give other people the opportunity to learn and, yes, maybe even break a few dishes. This is how you grow your work associates, church members, and children in your family. Delegate. You will divide your sorrows and multiply your peace!

Shortly after the children of Israel escaped from their bondage in Egypt, Jethro, the wise and aged father-in-law of Moses, came out to visit his son-in-law in the desert. Here's the story from Exodus 18:18–24:

> So it was, on the next day, that Moses sat to judge the people; and the people stood before Moses from morning until evening. So when Moses' father-in-law saw all that he did for the people, he said, "What is this thing that you are doing for the people? Why do you alone sit, and all the people stand before you from morning until evening?"
>
> And Moses said to his father-in-law, "Because the people come to me to inquire of God. When they have a difficulty, they come to me, and I judge between one and another; and I make known the statutes of God and His laws."
>
> So Moses' father-in-law said to him, "The thing that you do is not good. Both you and these people who are with you will surely wear yourselves out. For this thing is too much for you; you are not able to perform it by yourself. Listen now to my voice; I will give you counsel, and God will be with you: Stand before God for the people, so that you may bring the difficulties to God. And you shall teach them the statutes and the laws and show them the way in which they must walk and the work they must do. Moreover, you shall select from all the people able men, such as fear God, men of truth, hating covetousness; and place such over them to be rulers

of thousands, rulers of hundreds, rulers of fifties, and rulers of tens. And let them judge the people at all times. Then it will be that every great matter they shall bring to you, but every small matter they themselves shall judge. So it will be easier for you, for they will bear the burden with you. If you do this thing, and God so commands you, then you will be able to endure, and all this people will also go to their place in peace."

So Moses heeded the voice of his father-in-law and did all that he had said.

Do you think delegating tasks is wrong? One of the Bible's greatest prophets also had to be convinced to do it. Yet it was only by delegating problems that Moses could eventually lead the nation from slavery to freedom.

Worry Silos

Have you ever heard the expression, "a lazy man's load"? That's me sometimes. I don't want to carry three bags to the car when I leave the supermarket, so I try to fit everything into one bag. What happens? The bag breaks and I have big mess in the parking lot. Or I try to carry everything from the car to the house in one load when I should really do it in three trips. But I'm too lazy to make three trips. So what happens? I drop something.

What's my point? Some people try to manage all of their worries at the same time, and they become overwhelmed. But we need to manage our worries in separate silos.

Here you have another important practice in handling worries: compartmentalize them.

When I come home from work, I do not bring my wife a bouquet of work-related worries. As far as possible, I try to leave my work troubles at the office—tasks that are undone, unwritten emails, problems to be solved, calls to be made. When I enter the door of the house, I consciously leave my work worries in a separate compartment and close the lid. I can't do much regarding those problems until the office opens again anyway, so why worry? When I come home, Karen will sometimes ask me how work was that day? I'm thinking to myself, *"Please don't open that box."* I might answer, "It was fairly average," because every day of work has its varied troubles.

You should close the lid and bring some peace into your family; instead, help your spouse with some of his or her troubles and lessen the load.

Likewise, try to leave your household and family worries at home when you go to work or school. You usually cannot resolve them in these environments, so close the lid and smile with your friends. In fact, you may not have very many friends if you are always unloading on them all of your troubles from every aspect of your life. Lock them in their proper compartments and then close the lid. Relax until the right time and place comes to address them.

With some of the bigger challenges, of course, you can confide in a few close friends—ask them to join you in prayer. But if you always unload all your troubles on everybody who casually asks you how you're doing, soon they will stop asking. And you'll start worrying about why you don't have any friends!

Chapter 11

Grace for Today

You will have many problems in life—no doubt about that. The Bible is clear about acknowledging this reality. God even uses troubles to teach us and to test us. We find in the book of Job, "Man is born to trouble, as the sparks fly upward" (Job 5:7). In a world full of evil, there's no avoiding problems.

The apostle Paul talks about "strengthening the souls of the disciples, exhorting them to continue in the faith, and saying, 'We must through many tribulations enter the kingdom of God'" (Acts 14:22). The word "tribulation" is related to the word "trouble." It's through trouble that we enter the kingdom. There is going to be trouble, there are going to be problems, but God does not want you to worry about them. He doesn't want them to consume your thoughts and your time; He wants you to learn to trust Him *through* life's difficulties.

Jesus laid out the reality perfectly when He said, "These things I have spoken to you, that in Me you may have peace. In the world you will have tribulation; but be of good cheer, I have overcome the world" (John 16:33).

When problems threaten to overflow your life, seeking God will transport you to the safety of higher ground. "For this cause everyone who is godly shall pray to You in a time when You may be found; surely in a flood of great waters they shall not come near him" (Psalm 32:6).

The children of Israel came to a point in which things looked hopeless. They were at the shores of the Red Sea, with mountains on both sides of them and an army of angry Egyptians charging them from behind. They were unarmed. And they started to worry, crying out, "What do we do?"

Do you know what God told them? "*Do not be afraid.* Stand still, and see the salvation of the Lord, which He will accomplish for you today" (Exodus 14:13, my emphasis). God allowed the trouble to come close that they might develop trust in Him. And what was the outcome? God miraculously delivered His people. "He led them on safely, so that they did not fear; but the sea overwhelmed their enemies" (Psalm 78:53).

After we have done what we can to address whatever needs or problems we face, we've got to trust the Lord to do all the rest. He will give us grace and wisdom for that day's problems.

In Deuteronomy 33:25, we read, "Your sandals shall be iron and bronze." That sounds kind of uncomfortable, doesn't it? But it means that the sandals won't wear out, just as the Hebrews' footwear didn't wear out as they wandered through the wilderness. The verse continues—and here is what we especially need to notice: "As your days, so shall your strength be." God is not going to give you Herculean strength for today that you really don't need until tomorrow. When the challenge comes, He gives you the strength.

Jesus, in His Sermon on the Mount, got right to the point: "Do not worry about tomorrow, for tomorrow will worry about its own things" (Matthew 6:34). He commands us to not worry because worry wears away the lifeforce within; it robs us of our joy as Christians.

Someone once said that worry brings tomorrow's difficulties into today. God doesn't give you grace for tomorrow's difficulties. He gives you grace for today. Again, worry does not take the sorrow out of tomorrow; it only adds more sorrow today. And so, worry overloads us with trouble and sorrow; it's debilitating.

People have asked me, "Do you think you have enough faith?" You've probably wondered this yourself. If you are persecuted for your faith, do you have enough faith such that you would not deny Jesus?

My answer is, "Not today, I don't."

But when that day comes, my prayer is that I will have the faith to receive God's strength. So I'm not going to worry about that now because "as your days, so shall your strength be." We shouldn't say, "Lord, give me this *month* my *monthly* bread." We need to ask, "Give me this *day* my *daily* bread."

George McDonald, the famous Christian minister, advised, "Few men sink under the burden of the day. It's when tomorrow's burden is added to the burden of today, the weight is more than a man can bear. Never load yourself so." It's one thing to be concerned about the needs of the day, but if you start worrying *today* about all the future days, it can become a crushing load.

Now, I don't know about you, but I think that if anyone had anything to worry about, it would have been Jesus. Can you imagine knowing from twelve years of age that you were going to be the sacrifice for the world? And even if that information had been revealed to Him only at age thirty, when He began His preaching ministry, can you imagine going through more than three years of knowing? *"I am going to be punished for the sins of the whole world. I am going to suffer and be tortured. I am going to be placed into the hands of the devil."*

How would you feel knowing that every day was another day closer to the cross?

You'll notice that Jesus didn't let that bother Him. He didn't worry ahead. He did not really address concern for that event until that day arrived. It was only when He reached the garden in Gethsemane that He took it up, and it was a tremendous load for Him to bear, indeed. But He had slept through storms. The disciples woke Him up in terror, but He said, "What are you worried about?" He had complete peace in God's plan for Him.

Even the Roman ruler Pilate marveled when Jesus was brought before him. *"What's this person made of? He's about to be crucified, and He's not afraid?"* Pilate was so befuddled, He asked whether Jesus actually knew anything. He said, "Do You not know that I have power?" (John 19:10).

And Jesus answered, "You could have no power at all against Me unless it had been given you from above" (v. 11). Jesus wasn't worried. We need to follow His example.

After all, shouldn't Christians try to imitate Christ? One reason people were attracted to Jesus was His peace. He wants us to have the same kind of peace that passes understanding, not just for ourselves, but so that others will be drawn to Him as well.

What's the Worst That Can Happen?

Here's another important trick to easing your anxiety: Keep the big picture perspective. Ask the honest question, "What's the worst thing that could happen?" Statistically, we have learned, most of the things that people worry about are relatively inconsequential.

You're cramming for a driving test at 2:30 AM, worried that you might fail. Just ask yourself: What's the worst thing that can happen? Let's say you fail the test and have to take it again. Well, that's not exactly the end of the world—is it? You're probably not going to be barred from driving for the rest of your life.

As mentioned earlier, one of the most common fears people worry about is speaking in public. You're worried that you might stutter, stumble, freeze up, or say something silly or embarrassing. So what? What's the worst thing that could happen? You will probably be the only one thinking about your flub an hour after you talk. It's not worth stressing over.

Even with more serious problems, we can still ask the question. You learn from the doctor that you have cancer. Now that is serious. But think about it: The worst thing that can happen is that you will die. Keep in mind, that's going to happen to you eventually anyway if the Lord tarries. But should it worry a believer? You go to sleep—then wake up in the resurrection with a glorified body and no possibility of ever getting sick again.

How do you think Peter could sleep peacefully while bound in a Roman jail and scheduled to be executed in the morning? (See Acts 12.) How could Daniel sleep peacefully in a den full of lions?

And on the verge of his execution by Nero, Paul triumphantly wrote, "The time of my departure is at hand. I have fought the good fight, I have finished the race, I have kept the faith. Finally, there is laid up for me the crown of righteousness, which the Lord, the righteous Judge, will give to me on that Day" (2 Timothy 4:6–8).

Anxious for Nothing

What can you do about worry? The Bible has the answer. I briefly quoted earlier from Paul's words in the book of Philippians, giving us the perfect advice: "Be anxious for nothing" (4:6). Don't be worried about *how much?* He said don't be worried about *anything.*

This doesn't mean don't *think* about anything. Again, we need to understand the difference. You can ponder something without worrying about that something. Sometimes you will need to think things over, and that's okay. The Bible says don't be anxious. Don't take on the stress of things you can't change. Don't let it choke you. Don't be anxious for *anything.*

And the passage goes on: "But in everything by prayer and supplication." Here's another key: You need to bring your concerns to the Lord. He is waiting to help you. Martin Luther has been quoted as saying, "Pray, and let God worry." It's excellent advice whether he really said it or not!

But remember that you need to ask. Jesus said, "Ask, and it will be given to you" (Matthew 7:7). The apostle James wrote, "You do not have because you do not ask" (James 4:2). When we come to God and humbly ask for His help, He will provide. He may not provide for you in the way you think or expect, but in His perfect wisdom, He will provide whatever is best.

Next, returning to the passage in Philippians, the Bible says that we should ask "with thanksgiving." You should be grateful for what you already have. You need to maintain an attitude of gratitude.

Then, after the instructions, we find the promise: "Let your requests be made known to God; and the peace of God, which surpasses all understanding, will guard your hearts and minds through Christ Jesus" (Philippians 4:6, 7). Amen!

The University of Chicago once did a study about anxiety and came to the conclusion that listing out your concerns on paper could help decrease worry. "It might be counterintuitive, but it's almost as if you empty the fears out of your mind," study researcher Sian Beilock, an associate professor in psychology, told *U.S. News*. So science confirms it. Write down your worries and then present them to the Lord. You may experience some immediate relief!

Again, these are practical things you can do to handle your anxiety. Pray about your concerns; perhaps even make a list and present them before God, asking for His help while being grateful for the blessings He has already given you. Then be prepared to receive His peace into your heart. Believe the promises of God. Believe He's with you. Believe He's in control. No matter what the problem is, God has an answer for your need.

Let's look at another promise, one found in Romans 8:28:

> We know that all things work together for good to those who love God, to those who are the called according to His purpose.

How many things? *All* things. God can even take our mistakes, tragedies, or bad circumstances—things that are not in His will—and cause them to work for our good in miraculous ways, ways that we could never imagine.

We need to claim the promises of God and make them a foundation in our lives. Consider Jeremiah 29:11, for instance:

> I know the thoughts that I think toward you, says the Lord, thoughts of peace and not of evil, to give you a future and a hope.

Sometimes we're tempted to think, *"Oh, God, this is it—this is the one thing that's going to do me in."* But, through His promises, God reassures us, "No, I'm going to take care of you. Don't worry."

Peter wrote, "Humble yourselves under the mighty hand of God, that He may exalt you in due time, casting all your care"—what percentage of our care? Twenty-five percent? *I'm worried, Lord, that You're not worrying enough, so I need to worry about some of it.* But the Scripture says, "casting *all* your care upon Him"—that's 100 percent. Why? Because "He cares for you" (1 Peter 5:6, 7).

Perhaps you have heard this little poem:

> It is His will that I should cast my care on Him each day.
> He also bids me not to cast my confidence away.
> But, oh, how foolishly I act when taken unaware.
> I cast away my confidence and carry all my care.

Sometimes that's what we do because it's a natural tendency. But that's not what our heavenly Father wants for us.

Seeking His Kingdom

Another key to overcoming worry is going back to Matthew 6:33, where Jesus gives us a critical solution: "Seek first the kingdom of God and His righteousness." Our priority should be to do the work of His kingdom—to share the gospel with others.

We need to make it our goal to seek His kingdom in our lives, His righteousness in our hearts, and His kingdom around us, that others may also accept His salvation. He says that if we make it our central priority to build up His kingdom, "all these things shall be added to you." What are "these things"? The things He mentioned that people worry about!

Now your worry may not be centered about food. It may not be about clothes. It may not be about shelter. But whatever it is, He invites you to seek His kingdom first, casting all your cares upon Him, and all these other needs you have will be added. "I'll take care of the basics," He promises. "I'll take care of what you actually need." And this is where He adds, "Therefore do not worry about tomorrow, for tomorrow will worry about its own things. Sufficient for the day is its own trouble" (v. 34).

The Bottom Line

When I write on just about any subject, most of the time, I'm writing to myself. And, yes, I worry just like you worry. Hence, this book is also to remind me of these principles.

But we all have two choices each day: Are we going to worry? Or are we going to worship? Are we going to live by faith, like the birds and the flowers, living for the glory of God, trusting Him even though we don't see Him? Or are we going to put all our energy into worrying about what we can't change?

Would it make you feel better if God would just whisper in your ear, "I know about all the things you're dealing with right now. Don't worry; I've got it covered." Well, He's whispering that in your ear right now. And He has already "whispered" these things in your ear through His Word. I'm not the one who is saying these thing—Jesus is! He Himself has said to you, "Don't worry." He wants you to have His peace in your heart.

Robert Lewis Stevenson, the novelist, once wrote about sailors who were on a large ship in a terrible storm—not far from a dangerous rocky coast. If it weren't bad enough that they were afraid of being bashed on the rocks, they were also afraid that the massive waves were going to sink the boat. Several of the crew were down in the hold unable to sleep. In the violence of the storm, their hammocks were being thrown around and were slapping against the sides of the ship. The men were terrified that they were about to go under at any moment. Wouldn't you be?

Finally, one of them could take it no longer. With the ship pitching and tossing, he staggered up the stairs, hanging on to the railing as he crossed the deck, and made his way to the pilot house. As the sailor opened the door, he saw the captain at the helm, his calm face illuminated by a swinging kerosene lamp. The captain heard the door open, felt the wind rush in, so he turned to look at the sailor.

The captain knew the sailor was scared, so he gave him a big calm smile and turned back to steering the ship. The sailor didn't say anything. He shut the door, struggled back downstairs, and got together with his mates. They asked him what the captain had said. He answered, "He didn't say anything, but I know we have nothing to worry about."

"How do you know?" they asked.

He said, "I've seen the captain's face, and the captain's not worried."

Is God worried? Is He biting His nails? Is His brow furrowed and twisted with anxiety? Is He worried about your problems? If you're His child, and if He's not worried, then why are *you* worried? Look into the peaceful face of Jesus, friend.

I remember hearing about a businessman who was sitting on an airplane preparing for takeoff. The flight attendant brought by a young boy who was traveling alone and seated him in an empty seat next to the businessman. As she was buckling him in, it became evident this was the first time the boy had ever flown. The businessman could tell the wide-eyed young boy was nervous—especially after the flight attendant gave the regular safety drill about how to find the exits and put on a life preserver in the event of an emergency.

As the plane was taxiing and the engines began to roar before take-off, he saw that the little fellow's hands were clinging to the armrests, his knuckles flush white.

The man looked down at the boy's obvious uneasiness and said, "This is my favorite part. Isn't this fun?" The jet began to accelerate up the runway, creaking and rattling, until it rose into the air. The anxious boy looked up and saw the man smiling and showing so much excitement, he thought, *Oh, yeah, this is fun!* He relaxed immediately.

If you're traveling with your heavenly Father and He's not worried, why are you worried? He's at the controls. Just as He has taken care of you throughout your life—that's why you're still here—I'm pretty safe in saying that, one by one, He will take care of your problems as you bring them to Him.

Pray for wisdom, pray for grace, pray for the practical answers you need—whatever things you need to pray for, and pray for energy to do your part—but then leave it with God. He doesn't want you to go through life choked by worry. He will take care of you.

> Come to Me, all you who labor and are heavy laden, and I will give you rest. Take My yoke upon you and learn from Me, for I am gentle and lowly in heart, and you will find rest for your souls. For My yoke is easy and My burden is light (Matthew 11:28–30).

The most powerful being in the universe is your best friend. Jesus truly cares for *you.*

A Quick Reference List for Coping with Worry

If you're a chronic worrier, here's an emergency reference list for anxiety attacks. You may want to snap a picture of this and carry it around with you.

1. Pray, casting your cares upon God. Make a list of your worries and spread them out before God.
2. Count your blessings! Remember how God has taken care of you in the past.
3. Develop a practical plan to resolve your problems. Sometimes doing nothing will be the plan!
4. Compartmentalize worries. Store your distinct problems—school, work, and family—in separate silos until you can address them.
5. Lighten your load by delegating and sharing responsibilities.
6. Be content with what you already have and in the talents God has given you.
7. Sing a positive song or listen to uplifting music.
8. Focus on that which is good. Avoid negative news and chronically negative people.

9. Get some exercise, preferably out in God's nature.
10. Laugh! Read something funny and cultivate your sense of humor.
11. Eat healthy, exercise, and breathe deeply.
12. Assuming you're healthy and comfortable, enjoy the present.
13. Help someone else with their needs instead of fixating on your own.
14. Remember that an all-powerful God already knows the solution to your problem—and He is not worried. Rest in that truth!